ANCIENT ART AND RITUAL

Ancient Art and Ritual

JANE ELLEN HARRISON

GREENWOOD PRESS, PUBLISHERS
NEW YORK

PREFATORY NOTE

IT may be well at the outset to say clearly what is the aim of the present volume. The title is *Ancient Art and Ritual,* but the reader will find in it no general summary or even outline of the facts of either ancient art or ancient ritual. These facts are easily accessible in handbooks. The point of my title and the real gist of my argument lie perhaps in the word "*and*"—that is, in the intimate connection which I have tried to show exists between ritual and art. This connection has, I believe, an important bearing on questions vital to-day, as, for example, the question of the place of art in our modern civilization, its relation to and its difference from religion and morality; in a word, on the whole enquiry as to what the nature of art is and how it can help or hinder spiritual life.

I have taken Greek drama as a typical instance, because in it we have the clear historical case of a great art, which arose out of a very primitive and almost world-wide ritual. The rise of the Indian drama, or the mediæval and from it the modern stage, would have told us the same tale and served the like purpose. But Greece is nearer to us to-day than either India or the Middle Ages.

Greece and the Greek drama remind me that I should like to offer my thanks to Professor Gilbert Murray, for help and criticism which has far outrun the limits of editorial duty.

J. E. H.

Newnham College,
  Cambridge, June 1913.

NOTE TO THE FIFTH IMPRESSION

The original text has been reprinted without change except for the correction of misprints. A few additions (enclosed in square brackets) have been made to the Bibliography.

1947

CONTENTS

vii

ANCIENT ART AND RITUAL

CHAPTER I

ART AND RITUAL

THE title of this book may strike the reader
as strange and even dissonant. What have
art and ritual to do together ? The ritualist
is, to the modern mind, a man concerned
perhaps unduly with fixed forms and ceremonies, with carrying out the rigidly prescribed ordinances of a church or sect. The
artist, on the other hand, we think of as free
in thought and untrammelled by convention in
practice; his tendency is towards licence. Art
and ritual, it is quite true, have diverged
to-day; but the title of this book is chosen
advisedly. Its object is to show that these
two divergent developments have a common
root, and that neither can be understood
without the other. It is at the outset one

9

and the same impulse that sends a man to
church and to the theatre.

Such a statement may sound to-day para-
doxical, even irreverent. But to the Greek
of the sixth, fifth, and even fourth century B.C.,
it would have been a simple truism. We
shall see this best by following an Athenian
to his theatre, on the day of the great Spring
Festival of Dionysos.

Passing through the entrance-gate to the
theatre on the south side of the Acropolis,
our Athenian citizen will find himself at once
on holy ground. He is within a *temenos* or
precinct, a place " cut off " from the common
land and dedicated to a god. He will pass to
the left (Fig. 2, p. 144) two temples standing
near to each other, one of earlier, the other of
later date, for a temple, once built, was so
sacred that it would only be reluctantly
destroyed. As he enters the actual theatre
he will pay nothing for his seat ; his attendance
is an act of worship, and from the social point
of view obligatory ; the entrance fee is therefore paid for him by the State.

The theatre is open to all Athenian citizens,
but the ordinary man will not venture to

seat himself in the front row. In the front row, and that only, the seats have backs, and the central seat of this row is an armchair; the whole of the front row is permanently reserved, not for individual rich men who can afford to hire " boxes,"¹ but for certain State officials, and these officials are all priests. On each seat the name of the owner is inscribed; the central seat is " of the priest of Dionysos Eleuthereus," the god of the precinct. Near him is the seat " of the priest of Apollo the Laurel-Bearer," and again " of the priest of Asklepios," and " of the priest of Olympian Zeus," and so on round the whole front semicircle. It is as though at His Majesty's the front row of stalls was occupied by the whole bench of bishops, with the Archbishop of Canterbury enthroned in the central stall.

The theatre at Athens is not open night by night, nor even day by day. Dramatic performances take place only at certain high festivals of Dionysos in winter and spring. It is, again, as though the modern theatre was open only at the festivals of the Epiphany and of Easter. Our modern, at least our Protestant, custom is in direct contrast. We tend on great religious festivals rather to close than to open our theatres. Another point of contrast is in the time allotted to the performance. We give to the theatre our after-dinner hours, when work is done, or at best a couple of hours in the afternoon. The theatre is for us a recreation. The Greek theatre opened at sunrise, and the whole day was consecrated to high and strenuous religious attention. During the five or six days of the great *Dionysia*, the whole city was in a state of unwonted sanctity, under a *taboo*. To distrain a debtor was illegal; any personal assault, however trifling, was sacrilege.

Most impressive and convincing of all is the ceremony that took place on the eve of the performance. By torchlight, accompanied by a great procession, the image of the god Dionysos himself was brought to the theatre and placed in the orchestra. Moreover, he came not only in human but in animal form. Chosen young men of the Athenians in the flower of their youth—*epheboi*—escorted to the precinct a splendid bull. It was expressly ordained that the bull should be " worthy of the god "; he was, in fact, as we shall presently see, the primitive incarnation of the god. It is, again, as though in our modern theatre there stood, " sanctifying all things to our use and us to His service," the human figure of the Saviour, and beside him the Paschal Lamb.

But now we come to a strange thing. A god presides over the theatre, to go to the theatre is an act of worship to the god Dionysos, and yet, when the play begins, three times out of four of Dionysos we hear nothing. We see, it may be, Agamemnon returning from Troy, Clytemnestra waiting to slay him, the vengeance of Orestes, the love of Phædra for Hippolytos, the hate of Medea and the slaying of her children: stories beautiful, tragic, morally instructive it may be, but scarcely, we feel, religious. The orthodox Greeks themselves sometimes complained that in the plays enacted before them there was "nothing to do with Dionysos."

If drama be at the outset divine, with its roots in ritual, why does it issue in an art profoundly solemn, tragic, yet purely human ? The actors wear ritual vestments like those of the celebrants at the Eleusinian mysteries.

Why, then, do we find them, not executing a
religious service or even a drama of gods and
goddesses, but rather impersonating mere
Homeric heroes and heroines ?   Greek drama,
which seemed at first to give us our clue, to
show us a real link between ritual and art,
breaks down, betrays us, it would seem, just
at the crucial moment, and leaves us with our
problem on our hands.

Had we only Greek ritual and art we might
well despair.   The Greeks are a people of
such swift constructive imagination that
they almost always obscure any problem of
origins.   So fair and magical are their cloud-
capp'd towers that they distract our minds
from the task of digging for foundations.   There
is scarcely a problem in the origins of Greek
mythology and religion that has been solved
within the domain of Greek thinking only.
Ritual with them was, in the case of drama,
so swiftly and completely transmuted into
art that, had we had Greek material only to
hand, we might never have marked the transition.   Happily, however, we are not confined
within the Greek paradise.   Wider fields
are open to us; our subject is not only Greek,
but ancient art and ritual.   We can turn at

once to the Egyptians, a people slower-witted than the Greeks, and watch their sluggish but more instructive operatious. To one who is studying the development of the human mind the average or even stupid child is often more illuminating than the abnormally brilliant. Greece is often too near to us, too advanced, too modern, to be for comparative purposes instructive.

Of all Egyptian, perhaps of all ancient deities, no god has lived so long or had so wide and deep an influence as Osiris. He stands as the prototype of the great class of resurrection-gods who die that they may live again. His sufferings, his death, and his resurrection were enacted year by year in a great mystery-play at Abydos. In that mystery-play was set forth, first, what the Greeks call his *agon*, his contest with his enemy Set; then his *pathos*, his suffering, or downfall and defeat, his wounding, his death, and his burial; finally, his resurrection and " recognition," his *anagnorisis* either as himself or as his only begotten son Horus. Now the meaning of this thrice-told tale we shall consider later: for the moment we are concerned only with the fact that it is set forth both in art and ritual.

At the festival of Osiris small images of the god were made of sand and vegetable earth, his cheek bones were painted green and his face yellow. The images were cast in a mould of pure gold, representing the god as a mummy. After sunset on the 24th day of the month Choiak, the effigy of Osiris was laid in a grave and the image of the previous year was removed. The intent of all this was made transparently clear by other rites. At the beginning of the festival there was a ceremony of ploughing and sowing. One end of the field was sown with barley, the other with spelt; another part with flax. While this was going on the chief priest recited the ritual of the " sowing of the fields." Into the " garden " of the god, which seems to have been a large pot, were put sand and barley, then fresh living water from the inundation of the Nile was poured out of a golden ꝟ over the " garden " and the barley was lowed to grow up. It was the symbol of the resurrection of the god after his burial, " for the growth of the garden is the growth of the divine substance."

The death and resurrection of the gods,
and *pari passu* of the life and fruits of the
earth, was thus set forth in ritual, but—and
this is our immediate point—it was also set
forth in definite, unmistakable art.   In the
great temple of Isis at Philæ there is a chamber
dedicated to Osiris.   Here is represented the
dead Osiris.   Out of his body spring ears of
corn, and a priest waters the growing stalk
from a pitcher.   The inscription to the
picture reads : *This is the form of him whom
one may not name, Osiris of the mysteries, who
springs from the returning waters.*   It is but
another presentation of the ritual of the
month Choiak, in which effigies of the god
made of earth and corn were buried.   When
these effigies were taken up it would be found
that the corn had sprouted actually from the
body of the god, and this sprouting of the
grain would, as Dr. Frazer says, be " hailed
as an omen, or rather as the cause of the
growth of the crops." [1]

Even more vividly is the resurrection set
forth in the bas-reliefs that accompany the
great Osiris inscription at Denderah.   Here
the god is represented at first as a mummy

[1] *Adonis, Attis, Osiris,*[2] p. 324.

swathed and lying flat on his bier. Bit by
bit he is seen raising himself up in a series
of gymnastically impossible positions, till at
last he rises from a bowl—perhaps his
" garden "—all but erect, between the out-
spread wings of Isis, while before him a male
figure holds the *crux ansata*, the " cross with
a handle," the Egyptian symbol of life. In
ritual, the thing desired, *i. e.* the resurrection,
is acted, in art it is represented.

No one will refuse to these bas-reliefs the
title of art. In Egypt, then, we have clearly
an instance—only one out of many—where
art and ritual go hand in hand. Countless
bas-reliefs that decorate Egyptian tombs and
temples are but ritual practices translated
into stone. This, as we shall later see, is an
important step in our argument. Ancient
art and ritual are not only closely connected,
not only do they mutually explain and
illustrate each other, but, as we shall presently
find, they actually arise out of a common
human impulse.

The god who died and rose again is not of
course confined to Egypt; he is world-wide.
When Ezekiel (viii. 14) " came to the gate of

the Lord's house which was toward the
north " he beheld there the " women weeping
for Tammuz." This "abomination" the
house of Judah had brought with them from
Babylon. Tammuz is *Dumuzi*, "the true
son," or more fully, *Dumuzi-absu*, "true son
of the waters." He too, like Osiris, is a god
of the life that springs from inundation and
that dies down in the heat of the summer.
In Milton's procession of false gods,

" Thammuz came next behind,
Whose annual wound in Lebanon allured
The Syrian damsels to lament his fate
In amorous ditties all a summer's day."

Tammuz in Babylon was the young love of
Ishtar. Each year he died and passed below
the earth to the place of dust and death,
" the land from which there is no returning,
the house of darkness, where dust lies on door
and bolt." And the goddess went after him,
and while she was below, life ceased in the
earth, no flower blossomed and no child of
animal or man was born.

We know Tammuz, " the true son," best
by one of his titles, Adonis, the Lord or King.

The Rites of Adonis were celebrated at midsummer. That is certain and memorable; for, just as the Athenian fleet was setting sail on its ill-omened voyage to Syracuse, the streets of Athens were thronged with funeral processions, everywhere was seen the image of the dead god, and the air was full of the lamentations of weeping women. Thucydides does not so much as mention the coincidence, but Plutarch [1] tells us those who took account of omens were full of concern for the fate of their countrymen. To start an expedition on the day of the funeral rites of Adonis, the Canaanitish " Lord," was no luckier than to set sail on a Friday, the death-day of the " Lord " of Christendom.

The rites of Tammuz and of Adonis, celebrated in the summer, were rites of death rather than of resurrection. The emphasis is on the fading and dying down of vegetation rather than on its upspringing. The reason of this is simple and will soon become manifest. For the moment we have only to note that while in Egypt the rites of Osiris are represented as much by art as by ritual, in Babylon and Palestine in the feasts of Tammuz

[1] *Vit. Nik.*, 13.

and Adonis it is ritual rather than art that obtains.

We have now to pass to another enquiry. We have seen that art and ritual, not only in Greece but in Egypt and Palestine, are closely linked. So closely, indeed, are they linked that we even begin to suspect they may have a common origin. We have now to ask, what is it that links art and ritual so closely together, what have they in common ? Do they start from the same impulse, and if so why do they, as they develop, fall so widely asunder ?

It will clear the air if we consider for a moment what we mean by art, and also in somewhat greater detail what we mean by ritual.

Art, Plato [1] tells us in a famous passage of the *Republic*, is imitation; the artist imitates natural objects, which are themselves in his philosophy but copies of higher realities. All the artist can do is to make a copy of a copy, to hold up a mirror to Nature in which, as he turns it whither he will, " are reflected sun and heavens and earth and man," any-

[1] *Rep.* X, 596-9.

thing and everything. Never did a statement so false, so wrong-headed, contain so much suggestion of truth—truth which, by the help of analysing ritual, we may perhaps be able to disentangle. But first its falsehood must be grasped, and this is the more important as Plato's misconception in modified form lives on to-day. A painter not long ago thus defined his own art : " The art of painting is the art of imitating solid objects upon a flat surface by means of pigments." A sorry life-work ! Few people to-day, perhaps, regard art as the close and realistic copy of Nature; photography has at least scotched, if not slain, that error; but many people still regard art as a sort of improvement on or an " idealization " of Nature. It is the part of the artist, they think, to take suggestions and materials from Nature, and from these to build up, as it were, a revised version. It is, perhaps, only by studying those rudimentary forms of art that are closely akin to ritual that we come to see how utterly wrong-headed is this conception.

Take the representations of Osiris that we have just described—the mummy rising bit by bit from his bier. Can any one maintain

that art is here a copy or imitation of
reality ? However "realistic" the painting,
it represents a thing imagined not actual.
There never was any such person as Osiris,
and if there had been, he would certainly
never, once mummified, have risen from his
tomb. There is no question of fact, and the
copy of fact, in the matter. Moreover, had
there been, why should anyone desire to make
a copy of natural fact ? The whole "imitation" theory, to which, and to the element
of truth it contains, we shall later have
occasion to return, errs, in fact, through
supplying no adequate motive for a widespread human energy. It is probably this
lack of motive that has led other theorizers
to adopt the view that art is idealization. Man
with pardonable optimism desires, it is thought,
to improve on Nature.

Modern science, confronted with a problem
like that of the rise of art, no longer casts
about to conjecture how art *might* have arisen,
she examines how it actually *did* arise.
Abundant material has now been collected
from among savage peoples of an art so
primitive that we hesitate to call it art at

all, and it is in these inchoate efforts that we are able to track the secret motive springs that move the artist now as then.

Among the Huichol Indians,[1] if the people fear a drought from the extreme heat of the sun, they take a clay disk, and on one side of it they paint the " face " of Father Sun, a circular space surrounded by rays of red and blue and yellow which are called his " arrows," for the Huichol sun, like Phœbus Apollo, has arrows for rays. On the reverse side they will paint the progress of the sun through the four quarters of the sky. The journey is symbolized by a large cross-like figure with a central circle for midday. Round the edge are beehive-shaped mounds; these represent the hills of earth. The red and yellow dots that surround the hills are cornfields. The crosses on the hills are signs of wealth and money. On some of the disks birds and scorpions are painted, and on one are curving lines which mean rain. These disks are deposited on the altar of the god-house and left, and then all is well. The intention might

[1] C. H. Lumholtz, *Symbolism of the Huichol Indians*, in *Mem. of the Am. Mus. of Nat. Hist.*, Vol. III, " Anthropology." (1900.)

be to us obscure, but a Huichol Indian would read it thus : " Father Sun with his broad shield (or ' face ') and his arrows rises in the east, bringing money and wealth to the Huichols. His heat and the light from his rays make the corn to grow, but he is asked not to interfere with the clouds that are gathering on the hills."

Now is this art or ritual ? It is both and neither. *We* distinguish between a form of prayer and a work of art and count them in no danger of confusion; but the Huichol goes back to that earlier thing, a *presentation*. He utters, expresses his thought about the sun and his emotion about the sun and his relation to the sun, and if " prayer is the soul's sincere desire " he has painted a prayer. It is not a little curious that the same notion comes out in the old Greek word for " prayer," *euchè*. The Greek, when he wanted help in trouble from the " Saviours," the Dioscuri, carved a picture of them, and, if he was a sailor, added a ship. Underneath he inscribed the word *euchè*. It was not to begin with a " vow " paid, it was a presentation of his strong inner desire, it was a sculptured prayer.

Ritual then involves *imitation ;* but does

not arise out of it. It desires to recreate an
emotion, not to reproduce an object. A rite
is, indeed, we shall later see (p. 42), a sort of
stereotyped action, not really practical, but
yet not wholly cut loose from practice, a
reminiscence or an anticipation of actual
practical doing; it is fitly, though not quite
correctly, called by the Greeks a *dromenon,*
" a thing done."

At the bottom of art, as its motive power
and its mainspring, lies, not the wish to
copy Nature or even improve on her—the
Huichol Indian does not vainly expend his
energies on an effort so fruitless—but rather
an impulse shared by art with ritual, the desire, that is, to utter, to give out a strongly
felt emotion or desire by representing, by
making or doing or enriching the object or
act desired. The common source of the art
and ritual of Osiris is the intense, world-
wide desire that the life of Nature which
seemed dead should live again. This common
emotional factor it is that makes art and
ritual in their beginnings well-nigh indistin-
guishable. Both, to begin with, copy an
act, but not at first for the sake of the copy.
Only when the emotion dies down and is

forgotten does the copy become an end in
itself, a mere mimicry.

It is this downward path, this sinking of
making to mimicry, that makes us now-a-days
think of ritual as a dull and formal thing.
Because a rite has ceased to be believed in,
it does not in the least follow that it will
cease to be *done*. We have to reckon with all
the huge forces of habit. The motor nerves,
once set in one direction, given the slightest
impulse tend always to repeat the same
reaction. We mimic not only others but
ourselves mechanically, even after all emotion
proper to the act is dead; and then because
mimicry has a certain ingenious charm, it
becomes an end in itself for ritual, even for art.

It is not easy, as we saw, to classify the
Huichol prayer-disks. As prayers they are
ritual, as surfaces decorated they are speci-
mens of primitive art. In the next chapter
we shall have to consider a kind of ceremony
very instructive for our point, but again not
very easy to classify—the pantomimic dances
which are, almost all over the world, so striking
a feature in savage social and religious life.
Are they to be classed as ritual or art ?

These pantomime dances lie, indeed, at the very heart and root of our whole subject, and it is of the first importance that before going further in our analysis of art and ritual, we should have some familiarity with their general character and gist, the more so as they are a class of ceremonies now practically extinct. We shall find in these dances the meeting-point between art and ritual, or rather we shall find in them the rude, inchoate material out of which both ritual and art, at least in one of its forms, developed. Moreover, we shall find in pantomimic dancing a ritual bridge, as it were, between actual life and those representations of life which we call art.

In our next chapter, therefore, we shall study the ritual dance in general, and try to understand its psychological origin; in the following chapter (III) we shall take a particular dance of special importance, the Spring Dance as practised among various primitive peoples. We shall then be prepared to approach the study of the Spring Dance among the Greeks, which developed into their drama, and thereby to, we hope, throw light on the relation between ritual and art.

CHAPTER II

IN books and hymns of bygone days, which dealt with the religion of " the heathen in his blindness," he was pictured as a being of strange perversity, apt to bow down to " gods of wood and stone." The question *why* he acted thus foolishly was never raised. It was just his " blindness "; the light of the gospel had not yet reached him. Now-a-days the savage has become material not only for conversion and hymn-writing but for scientific observation. We want to understand his psychology, *i. e.* how he behaves, not merely for his sake, that we may abruptly and despotically convert or reform him, but for our own sakes; partly, of course, for sheer love of knowing, but also,—since we realize that our own behaviour is based on instincts kindred to his,—in order that, by understanding his behaviour, we may understand, and it may be better, our own.

Anthropologists who study the primitive peoples of to-day find that the worship of false gods, bowing " down to wood and stone," bulks larger in the mind of the hymn-writer than in the mind of the savage. We look for temples to heathen idols; we find dancing-places and ritual dances. The savage is a man of action. Instead of asking a god to do what he wants done, he does it or tries to do it himself; instead of prayers he utters spells. In a word, he practises magic, and above all he is strenuously and frequently engaged in dancing magical dances. When a savage wants sun or wind or rain, he does not go to church and prostrate himself before a false god; he summons his tribe and dances a sun dance or a wind dance or a rain dance. When he would hunt and catch a bear, he does not pray to his god for strength to outwit and outmatch the bear, he rehearses his hunt in a bear dance.

Here, again, we have some modern prejudice and misunderstanding to overcome. Dancing is to us a light form of recreation practised by the quite young from sheer *joie de vivre*, and essentially inappropriate to the mature. But among the Tarahumares of Mexico the word

nolávoa means both " to work " and " to
dance." An old man will reproach a young
man saying, " Why do you not go and work ? "
(*nolávoa*). He means "Why do you not
dance instead of looking on ? " It is strange
to us to learn that among savages, as a man
passes from childhood to youth, from youth
to mature manhood, so the number of his
" dances " increase, and the number of these
" dances " is the measure *pari passu* of his
social importance. Finally, in extreme old
age he falls out, he ceases to exist, *because he
cannot dance ;* his dance, and with it his
social status, passes to another and a younger.

Magical dancing still goes on in Europe to-
day. In Swabia and among the Transylvanian
Saxons it is a common custom, says Dr. Frazer,[1]
for a man who has some hemp to leap high
in the field in the belief that this will make
the hemp grow tall. In many parts of
Germany and Austria the peasant thinks he
can make the flax grow tall by dancing or
leaping high or by jumping backwards from
a table; the higher the leap the taller will

[1] These instances are all taken from *The Golden Bough.*³
The Magic Art, I, 139 ff.

be the flax that year. There is happily little
possible doubt as to the practical reason
of this mimic dancing. When Macedonian
farmers have done digging their fields they
throw their spades up into the air and, catch-
ing them again, exclaim, " May the crop grow
as high as the spade has gone." In some
parts of Eastern Russia the girls dance one
by one in a large hoop at midnight on Shrove
Tuesday. The hoop is decked with leaves,
flowers and ribbons, and attached to it are
a small bell and some flax. While dancing
within the hoop each girl has to wave her
arms vigorously and cry, " Flax, grow," or
words to that effect. When she has done
she leaps out of the hoop or is lifted out of it
by her partner.

Is this art ? We shall unhesitatingly
answer " No." Is it ritual ? With some
hesitation we shall probably again answer
" No." It is, we think, not a rite, but merely
a superstitious practice of ignorant men
and women. But take another instance.
Among the Omaha Indians of North America,
when the corn is withering for want of rain,
the members of the sacred Buffalo Society fill
a large vessel with water and dance four times

round it. One of them drinks some of the water and spirts it into the air, making a fine spray in imitation of mist or drizzling rain. Then he upsets the vessel, spilling the water on the ground; whereupon the dancers fall down and drink up the water, getting mud all over their faces. This saves the corn. Now probably any dispassionate person would describe such a ceremonial as " an interesting instance of primitive *ritual*." The sole differ-ence between the two types is that, in the one the practice is carried on privately, or at least unofficially, in the other it is done publicly by a collective authorized body, officially for the public good.

The distinction is one of high importance, but for the moment what concerns us is, to see the common factor in the two sets of acts, what is indeed their source and mainspring. In the case of the girl dancing in the hoop and leaping out of it there is no doubt. The words she says, " Flax, grow," prove the point. She *does* what she *wants done*. Her intense desire finds utterance in an act. She obeys the simplest possible impulse. Let any-one watch an exciting game of tennis, or better still perhaps a game of billiards, he

will find himself *doing* in sheer sympathy the
thing he wants done, reaching out a tense arm
where the billiard cue should go, raising an
unoccupied leg to help the suspended ball over
the net. Sympathetic magic is, modern
psychology teaches us, in the main and at the
outset, not the outcome of intellectual illusion,
not even the exercise of a " mimetic instinct,"
but simply, in its ultimate analysis, an utterance, a discharge of emotion and longing.

But though the utterance of emotion is the
prime and moving, it is not the sole, factor.
We may utter emotion in a prolonged howl,
we may even utter it in a collective prolonged
howl, yet we should scarcely call this ritual,
still less art. It is true that a prolonged
collective howl will probably, because it is
collective, develop a rhythm, a regular recurrence, and hence probably issue in a kind of
ritual music; but for the further stage of development into art another step is necessary.
We must not only *utter* emotion, we must
represent it, that is, we must in some way
reproduce or imitate or express the thought
which is causing us emotion. Art is not
imitation, but art and also ritual frequently
and legitimately *contain an element of imita-*

tion. Plato was so far right. What exactly is imitated we shall see when we come to discuss the precise difference between art and ritual.

The Greek word for a *rite* as already noted is *dromenon,* "a thing done "—and the word is full of instruction. The Greek had realized that to perform a rite you must *do* something, that is, you must not only feel something but express it in action, or, to put it psychologically, you must not only receive an impulse, you must react to it. The word for rite, *dromenon,* "thing done," arose, of course, not from any psychological analysis, but from the simple fact that rites among the primitive Greeks were *things done,* mimetic dances and the like. It is a fact of cardinal importance that their word for theatrical representation, *drama,* is own cousin to their word for rite, *dromenon ; drama* also means "thing done." Greek linguistic instinct pointed plainly to the fact that art and ritual are near relations. To this fact of crucial importance for our argument we shall return later. But from the outset it should be borne in mind that in these two Greek words, *dromenon* and *drama*, in their exact meaning, their relation and their distinction, we have the keynote and clue to our whole discussion.

For the moment we have to note that the Greek word for rite, *dromenon*, " thing done," is not strictly adequate. It omits a factor of prime importance; it includes too much and not enough. All " things done " are not rites. You may shrink back from a blow; that is the expression of an emotion, that is a reaction to a stimulus, but that is not a rite. You may digest your dinner; that is a thing done, and a thing of high importance, but it is not a rite.

One element in the rite we have already observed, and that is, that it be done collectively, by a number of persons feeling the same emotion. A meal digested alone is certainly no rite; a meal eaten in common, under the influence of a common emotion, may, and often does, *tend* to become a rite.

Collectivity and emotional tension, two elements that tend to turn the simple reaction into a rite, are—specially among primitive peoples—closely associated, indeed scarcely separable. The individual among savages has but a thin and meagre personality; high emotional tension is to him only caused and maintained by a thing felt socially; it is what the tribe feels that is sacred, that is matter for ritual. He may make by himself excited movements, he may leap for joy, for fear; but unless these movements are made by the tribe together they will not become rhythmical; they will probably lack intensity, and certainly permanence. Intensity, then, and collectivity go together, and both are necessary for ritual, but both may be present without constituting art; we have not yet touched the dividing line between art and ritual. When and how does the *dromenon*, the *rite done*, pass over into the *drama* ?

The genius of the Greek language *felt*, before it consciously *knew*, the difference. This feeling ahead for distinctions is characteristic of all languages, as has been well shown by Mr. Pearsall Smith [1] in another manual of our series. It is an instinctive process arising independently of reason, though afterwards justified by it. What, then, is the distinction between art and ritual which the genius of the

[1] "The English Language," *Home University Library*, p. 28.

Greek language felt after, when it used the two words *dromenon* and *drama* for two different sorts of " things done " ?   To answer our question we must turn for a brief moment to psychology, the science of human behaviour.

We are accustomed for practical convenience to divide up our human nature into partitions—intellect, will, the emotions, the passions—with further subdivisions, *e. g.* of the intellect into reason, imagination, and the like.   These partitions we are apt to arrange into a sort of order of merit or as it is called a hierarchy, with Reason as head and crown, and under her sway the emotions and passions.   The result of establishing this hierarchy is that the impulsive side of our nature comes off badly, the passions and even the emotions lying under a certain ban.   This popular psychology is really a convenient and perhaps indispensable mythology.   Reason, the emotions, and the will have no more separate existences than Jupiter, Juno, and Minerva.

A more fruitful way of looking at our human constitution is to see it, not as a bundle of separate faculties, but as a sort of continuous cycle of activities. What really happens is, putting it very roughly, something of this sort. To each one of us the world is, or seems to be, eternally divided into two halves. On the one side is ourself, on the other all the rest of things. All our action, our behaviour, our life, is a relation between these two halves, and that behaviour seems to have three, not divisions, but stages. The outside world, the other half, the object if we like so to call it, acts upon us, gets at us through our senses. We hear or see or taste or feel something; to put it roughly, we perceive something, and as we perceive it, so, instantly, we feel about it, towards it, we have emotion. And, instantly again, that emotion becomes a motive-power, we re-act towards the object that got at us, we want to alter it or our relation to it. If we did not perceive we should not feel, if we did not feel we should not act. When we talk—as we almost must talk—of Reason, the Emotions, or the Passions and the Will leading to action, we think of the three stages or aspects of our behaviour as separable and even perhaps hostile ; we want, perhaps, to purge the intellect from all infection of the emotions. But in reality, though at a given moment one or the other element, knowing, feeling, or acting, may be dominant in our consciousness, the rest are always immanent.

When we think of the three elements or stages, knowing, feeling, striving, as all being necessary factors in any complete bit of human behaviour, we no longer try to arrange them in a hierarchy with knowing or reason at the head. Knowing—that is, receiving and recognizing a stimulus from without— would seem to come first; we must be acted on before we can *re*-act; but priority confers no supremacy. We can look at it another way. Perceiving is the first rung on the ladder that leads to action, feeling is the second, action is the topmost rung, the primary goal, as it were, of all the climbing. For the purpose of our discussion this is perhaps the simplest way of looking at human behaviour.

Movement, then, action, is, as it were, the goal and the end of thought. Perception finds its natural outlet and completion in doing. But here comes in a curious considera- tion important for our purpose. In animals, in so far as they act by " instinct," as we say, perception, knowing, is usually followed im-

mediately and inevitably by doing, by such
doing as is calculated to conserve the animal
and his species; but in some of the higher
animals, and especially in man, where the
nervous system is more complex, perception is
not instantly transformed into action; there is
an interval for choice between several possible
actions. Perception is pent up and becomes,
helped by emotion, conscious *representation*.
Now it is, psychologists tell us, just in this
interval, this space between perception and
reaction, this momentary halt, that all our
mental life, our images, our ideas, our consciousness, and assuredly our religion and our
art, is built up. If the cycle of knowing,
feeling, acting, were instantly fulfilled, that
is, if we were a mass of well-contrived instincts, we should hardly have *dromena*, and
we should certainly never pass from *dromena*
to *drama*. Art and religion, though perhaps
not wholly ritual, spring from the incomplete
cycle, from unsatisfied desire, from perception
and emotion that have somehow not found
immediate outlet in practical action. When
we come later to establish the dividing line
between art and ritual we shall find this fact
to be cardinal.

We have next to watch how out of *representation repeated* there grows up a kind of
abstraction which helps the transition from
ritual to art.   When the men of a tribe
return from a hunt, a journey, a battle,
or any event that has caused them keen
and pleasant emotion, they will often re-
act their doings round the camp-fire at
night to an attentive audience of women
and young boys.   The cause of this world-
wide custom is no doubt in great part
the desire to repeat a pleasant experience;
the battle or the hunt will not be re-enacted
unless it has been successful.   Together with
this must be reckoned a motive seldom absent
from human endeavour, the desire for self-
exhibition, self-enhancement.   But in this
re-enactment, we see at once, lies the germ of
history and of commemorative ceremonial,
and also, oddly enough, an impulse emotional
in itself begets a process we think of as
characteristically and exclusively intellectual,
the process of abstraction.   The savage begins
with the particular battle that actually *did*
happen; but, it is easy to see that if he re-
enacts it again and again the *particular* battle
or hunt will be forgotten, the representation

cuts itself loose from the particular action from which it arose, and becomes generalized, as it were abstracted. Like children he plays not at a funeral, but at " funerals," not at a battle, but at battles; and so arises the war-dance, or the death-dance, or the hunt-dance. This will serve to show how inextricably the elements of knowing and feeling are intertwined.

So, too, with the element of action. If we consider the occasions when a savage dances, it will soon appear that it is not only after a battle or a hunt that he dances in order to commemorate it, but before. Once the commemorative dance has got abstracted or generalized it becomes material for the magical dance, the dance pre-done. A tribe about to go to war will work itself up by a war dance; about to start out hunting they will catch their game in pantomime. Here clearly the main emphasis is on the practical, the active, doing-element in the cycle. The dance is, as it were, a sort of precipitated desire, a discharge of pent-up emotion into action.

In both these kinds of dances, the dance that commemorates by *re*-presenting and the dance that anticipates by *pre*-presenting, Plato would have seen the element of imitation,

what the Greeks called *mimesis*, which we saw
he believed to be the very source and essence
of all art.   In a sense he would have been right.
The commemorative dance does especially
re-present; it reproduces the past hunt or
battle; but if we analyse a little more closely
we see it is not for the sake of copying the
actual battle itself, but for the *emotion felt
about the battle*.   This they desire to re-live.
The emotional element is seen still more
clearly in the dance *fore*-done for magical
purposes.   Success in war or in the hunt is
keenly, intensely desired.   The hunt or the
battle cannot take place at the moment, so
the cycle cannot complete itself.   The desire
cannot find utterance in the actual act; it
grows and accumulates by inhibition, till at
last the exasperated nerves and muscles can
bear it no longer; it breaks out into mimetic
anticipatory action.   But, and this is the important point, the action is mimetic, not of what
you see done by another; but of what you
desire to do yourself.   The habit of this *mimesis*
of the thing desired, is set up, and ritual
begins.   Ritual, then, does imitate, but for an
emotional, not an altogether practical, end.

Plato never saw a savage war-dance or a
hunt-dance or a rain-dance, and it is not
likely that, if he had seen one, he would have
allowed it to be art at all. But he must often
have seen a class of performances very similar,
to which unquestionably he would give the
name of art. He must have seen plays like
those of Aristophanes, with the chorus dressed
up as Birds or Clouds or Frogs or Wasps, and
he might undoubtedly have claimed such plays
as evidence of the rightness of his definition.
Here were men *imitating* birds and beasts,
dressed in their skins and feathers, mimicking
their gestures. For his own days his judg-
ment would have been unquestionably right;
but again, if we look at the beginning of
things, we find an origin and an impulse
much deeper, vaguer, and more emotional.

The beast dances found widespread over the
savage world took their rise when men really
believed, what St. Francis tried to preach :
that beasts and birds and fishes were his
" little brothers." Or rather, perhaps, more
strictly, he felt them to be his great brothers
and his fathers, for the attitude of the Australian towards the kangaroo, the North
American towards the grizzly bear, is one of

affection tempered by deep religious awe. The beast dances look back to that early phase of civilization which survives in crystallized form in what we call *totemism*. " Totem " means tribe, but the tribe was of animals as well as men. In the Kangaroo tribe there were real leaping kangaroos as well as men-kangaroos. The men-kangaroos when they danced and leapt did it, not to *imitate* kangaroos—you cannot imitate yourself—but just for natural joy of heart because they *were* kangaroos ; they belonged to the Kangaroo tribe, they bore the tribal marks and delighted to assert their tribal unity. What they felt was not *mimesis* but " participation," unity, and community. Later, when man begins to distinguish between himself and his strange fellow-tribesmen, to realize that he is *not* a kangaroo like other kangaroos, he will try to revive his old faith, his old sense of participation and oneness, by conscious imitation. Thus though imitation is not the object of these dances, it grows up in and through them. It is the same with art. The origin of art is not *mimesis*, but *mimesis* springs up out of art, out of emotional expression, and constantly and closely neigh-

bours it.   Art and ritual are at the outset
alike in this, that they do not seek to copy a
fact, but to reproduce, to re-enact an emotion.

We shall see this more clearly if we examine
for a moment this Greek word *mimesis*.   We
translate mīmēsis by " imitation," and we
do very wrongly.   The word *mimesis* means
the action or doing of a person called a *mime*.
Now a *mime* was simply a person who dressed
up and acted in a pantomime or primitive
drama.   He was roughly what we should
call an *actor*, and it is significant that in the
word *actor* we stress not imitating but acting,
doing, just what the Greek stressed in his
words *dromenon* and *drama*.   The actor dresses
up, puts on a mask, wears the skin of a beast
or the feathers of a bird, not, as we have
seen, to copy something or some one who is
not himself, but to emphasize, enlarge, enhance, his own personality; he masquerades,
he does not mimic.

The celebrants in the very primitive ritual
of the Mountain-Mother in Thrace were, we
know, called *mimes*.   In the fragment of his
lost play, Æschylus, after describing the din
made by the " mountain gear " of the Mother,

the maddening hum of the *bombykes*, a sort of spinning-top, the clash of the brazen cymbals and the twang of the strings, thus goes on :

" And bull-voices roar thereto from somewhere out of the unseen, fearful *mimes*, and from a drum an image, as it were, of thunder underground is borne on the air heavy with dread."

Here we have undoubtedly some sort of "bull-roaring," thunder- and wind-making ceremony, like those that go on in Australia to-day. The *mimes* are not mimicking thunder out of curiosity, they are making it and enacting and uttering it for magical purposes. When a sailor wants a wind he makes it, or, as he later says, he whistles *for* it; when a savage or a Greek wants thunder to bring rain he makes it, becomes it. But it is easy to see that as the belief in magic declines, what was once intense desire, issuing in the making of or the being of a thing, becomes mere copying of it; the mime, the maker, sinks to be in our modern sense the mimic; as faith declines, folly and futility set in; the earnest, zealous *act* sinks into a frivolous mimicry, a sort of child's-play.

CHAPTER III

WE have seen in the last chapter that whatever interests primitive man, whatever makes him feel strongly, he tends to re-enact. Any one of his manifold occupations, hunting, fighting, later ploughing and sowing, provided it be of sufficient interest and importance, is material for a *dromenon* or rite. We have also seen that, weak as he is in individuality, it is not his private and personal emotions that tend to become ritual, but those that are public, felt and expressed officially, that is, by the whole tribe or community. It is further obvious that such dances, when they develop into actual rites, tend to be performed at fixed times. We have now to consider when and why. The element of fixity and regular repetition in rites cannot be too strongly emphasized. It is a factor of paramount importance, essential to the development from ritual to art, from *dromenon* to drama.

49

The two great interests of primitive man
are food and children. As Dr. Frazer has well
said, if man the individual is to live he must
have food; if his race is to persist he must
have children. " To live and to cause to
live, to eat food and to beget children,
these were the primary wants of man in the
past, and they will be the primary wants
of men in the future so long as the world
lasts." Other things may be added to enrich
and beautify human life, but, unless these
wants are first satisfied, humanity itself must
cease to exist. These two things, therefore,
food and children, were what men chiefly
sought to procure by the performance of
magical rites for the regulation of the seasons.
They are the very foundation-stones of that
ritual from which art, if we are right, took its
rise. From this need for food sprang seasonal,
periodic festivals. The fact that festivals are
seasonal, constantly recurrent, solidifies, makes
permanent, and as already explained (p. 42),
in a sense intellectualizes and abstracts the
emotion that prompts them.

The seasons are indeed only of value to
primitive man because they are related, as
he swiftly and necessarily finds out, to his

food supply. He has, it would seem, little sensitiveness to the æsthetic impulse of the beauty of a spring morning, to the pathos of autumn. What he realizes first and foremost is, that at certain times the animals, and still more the plants, which form his food, appear, at certain others they disappear. It is these times that become the central points, the focuses of his interest, and the dates of his religious festivals. These dates will vary, of course, in different countries and in different climates. It is, therefore, idle to attempt a study of the ritual of a people without knowing the facts of their climate and surroundings. In Egypt the food supply will depend on the rise and fall of the Nile, and on this rise and fall will depend the ritual and calendar of Osiris. And yet treatises on Egyptian religion are still to be found which begin by recounting the rites and mythology of Osiris, as though these were primary, and then end with a corollary to the effect that these rites and this calendar were " associated " with the worship of Osiris, or, even worse still, " instituted by " the religion of Osiris. The Nile regulates the food supply of Egypt, the monsoon that of certain South Pacific islands;

the calendar of Egypt depends on the Nile, of the South Pacific islands on the monsoon.

In his recent *Introduction to Mathematics* [1] Dr. Whitehead has pointed out how the "whole life of Nature is dominated by the existence of periodic events." The rotation of the earth produces successive days; the path of the earth round the sun leads to the yearly recurrence of the seasons; the phases of the moon are recurrent, and though artificial light has made these phases pass almost unnoticed to-day, in climates where the skies are clear, human life was largely influenced by moonlight. Even our own bodily life, with its recurrent heart-beats and breathings, is essentially periodic. [2] The presupposition of periodicity is indeed fundamental to our very conception of life, and but for periodicity the very means of measuring time as a quantity would be absent.

Periodicity is fundamental to certain departments of mathematics, that is evident; it is perhaps less evident that periodicity is a factor that has gone to the making of ritual, and hence, as we shall see, of art.

[1] Chapter XII: "Periodicity in Nature."　　[2] *Ibid.*

And yet this is manifestly the case. All primitive calendars are ritual calendars, successions of feast-days, a patchwork of days of different quality and character recurring; pattern at least is based on periodicity. But there is another and perhaps more important way in which periodicity affects and in a sense causes ritual. We have seen already that out of the space between an impulse and a reaction there arises an idea or " presentation." A " presentation " is, indeed, it would seem, in its final analysis, only a delayed, intensified desire—a desire of which the active satisfaction is blocked, and which runs over into a " presentation." An image conceived " presented," what we call an *idea* is, as it were, an act prefigured.

Ritual acts, then, which depend on the periodicity of the seasons are acts necessarily delayed. The thing delayed, expected, waited for, is more and more a source of value, more and more apt to precipitate into what we call an idea, which is in reality but the projected shadow of an unaccomplished action. More beautiful it may be, but comparatively bloodless, yet capable in its turn of acting as an initial motor impulse in the

cycle of activity. It will later (p. 70) be seen
that these periodic festivals are the stuff of
which those faded, unaccomplished actions
and desires which we call gods—Attis, Osiris,
Dionysos—are made.

To primitive man, as we have seen, beast
and bird and plant and himself were not
sharply divided, and the periodicity of the
seasons was for all. It will depend on man's
social and geographical conditions whether he
notices periodicity most in plants or animals.
If he is nomadic he will note the recurrent
births of other animals and of human children,
and will connect them with the lunar year.
But it is at once evident that, at least in
Mediterranean lands, and probably everywhere, it is the periodicity of plants and
vegetation generally which depends on moisture, that is most striking. Plants die down
in the heat of summer, trees shed their leaves
in autumn, all Nature sleeps or dies in winter,
and awakes in spring.

Sometimes it is the dying down that attracts
most attention. This is very clear in the rites
of Adonis, which are, though he rises again,
essentially rites of lamentation. The details

of the ritual show this clearly, and specially as already seen in the cult of Osiris. For the "gardens" of Adonis the women took baskets or pots filled with earth, and in them, as children sow cress now-a-days, they planted wheat, fennel, lettuce, and various kinds of flowers, which they watered and tended for eight days. In hot countries the seeds sprang up rapidly, but as the plants had no roots they withered quickly away. At the end of the eight days they were carried out with the images of the dead Adonis and thrown with them into the sea or into springs. The "gardens" of Adonis became the type of transient loveliness and swift decay.

" What waste would it be," says Plutarch,[1] " what inconceivable waste, for God to create man, had he not an immortal soul. He would be like the women who make little gardens, not less pleasant than the gardens of Adonis in earthen pots and pans; so would our souls blossom and flourish but for a day in a soft and tender body of flesh without any firm and solid root of life, and then be blasted and put out in a moment."

[1] *De Ser. Num.* 17.

Celebrated at midsummer as they were,
and as the " gardens " were thrown into water,
it is probable that the rites of Adonis may have
been, at least in part, a rain-charm. In the long
summer droughts of Palestine and Babylonia
the longing for rain must often have been
intense enough to provoke expression, and
we remember (p. 19) that the Sumerian
Tammuz was originally *Dumuzi-absu*, " True
Son of the Waters." Water is the first need
for vegetation. Gardens of Adonis are still
in use in the Madras Presidency.[1] At the
marriage of a Brahman " seeds of five or
nine sorts are mixed and sown in earthen pots
which are made specially for the purpose, and
are filled with earth. Bride and bridegroom
water the seeds both morning and evening for
four days; and on the fifth day the seedlings
are thrown, like the real gardens of Adonis,
into a tank or river."

Seasonal festivals with one and the same
intent—the promotion of fertility in plants,
animals and man—may occur at almost any
time of the year. At midsummer, as we have
seen, we may have rain-charms; in autumn
we shall have harvest festivals; in late autumn

[1] Frazer, *Adonis, Attis, and Osiris*,[3] p. 200.

and early winter among pastoral peoples we
shall have festivals, like that of Martinmas,
for the blessing and purification of flocks and
herds when they come in from their summer
pasture.   In midwinter there will be a Christ-
mas festival to promote and protect the sun's
heat at the winter solstice.   But in Southern
Europe, to which we mainly owe our drama
and our art, the festival most widely celebrated, and that of which we know most, is
the Spring Festival, and to that we must turn.
The spring is to the Greek of to-day the
"ánoixis," "the Opening," and it was in
spring and with rites of spring that both Greek
and Roman originally began their year. It was
this spring festival that gave to the Greek
their god Dionysos and in part his drama.

In Cambridge on May Day two or three
puzzled and weary little boys and girls are
still to be sometimes seen dragging round
a perambulator with a doll on it bedecked
with ribbons and a flower or two. That is
all that is left in most parts of England of
the Queen of the May and Jack-in-the-Green,
though here and there a maypole survives and
is resuscitated by enthusiasts about folk-

dances. But in the days of " Good Queen Bess " merry England, it would seem, was lustier. The Puritan Stubbs, in his *Anatomie of Abuses*,[1] thus describes the festival :

" They have twentie or fortie yoke of oxen, every oxe havyng a sweete nosegaie of flowers tyed on the tippe of his hornes, and these oxen draw home this Maiepoole (this stinckying idoll rather), which is covered all over with flowers and hearbes, bound round aboute with stringes from the top to the bottome, and sometyme painted with variable colours, with two or three hundred men, women, and children, following it with great devotion. And thus beyng reared up, with handkerchiefes and flagges streaming on the toppe, they strewe the ground about, binde greene boughs about it, set up summer haules, bowers, and arbours hard by it. And then fall they to banquet and feast, to leap and daunce aboute it, as the heathen people did at the dedication of their idolles, whereof this is a perfect patterne or rather the thyng itself."

The stern old Puritan was right, the maypole was the perfect pattern of a heathen

[1] Quoted by Dr. Frazer, *The Golden Bough*,[2] p. 203.

"idoll, or rather the thyng itself." He
would have exterminated it root and branch,
but other and perhaps wiser divines took the
maypole into the service of the Christian
Church, and still [1] on May Day in Saffron
Walden the spring song is heard with its
Christian moral—

"A branch of May we have brought you,
    And at your door it stands;
It is a sprout that is well budded out,
    The work of our Lord's hands."

The maypole was of course at first no pole
cut down and dried. The gist of it was that
it should be a "sprout, well budded out."
The object of carrying in the May was to
bring the very spirit of life and greenery into
the village. When this was forgotten, idleness
or economy would prompt the villagers to use
the same tree or branch year after year. In
the villages of Upper Bavaria Dr. Frazer [2] tells
us the maypole is renewed once every three,
four, or five years. It is a fir-tree fetched from
the forest, and amid all the wreaths, flags, and
inscriptions with which it is bedecked, an

[1] E. K. Chambers, *The Mediæval Stage*, I, p. 169.
[2] *The Golden Bough,*[2] p. 205.

essential part is the bunch of dark green
foliage left at the top, " as a memento that in
it we have to do, not with a dead pole, but
with a living tree from the greenwood."

⟩ At the ritual of May Day not only was
the fresh green bough or tree carried into the
village, but with it came a girl or a boy, the
Queen or King of the May. Sometimes
the tree itself, as in Russia, is dressed up in
woman's clothes; more often a real man or
maid, covered with flowers and greenery, walks
with the tree or carries the bough. Thus in
Thuringia,[1] as soon as the trees begin to be
green in spring, the children assemble on a
Sunday and go out into the woods, where
they choose one of their playmates to be
Little Leaf Man. They break branches from
the trees and twine them about the child, till
only his shoes are left peeping out. Two of
the other children lead him for fear he should
stumble. They take him singing and dancing
from house to house, asking for gifts of food,
such as eggs, cream, sausages, cakes. Finally,
they sprinkle the Leaf Man with water and
feast on the food. Such a Leaf Man is our
English Jack-in-the-Green, a chimney-sweeper

[1] *The Golden Bough,*[2] p. 213.

who, as late as 1892, was seen by Dr. Rouse walking about at Cheltenham encased in a wooden framework covered with greenery.

The bringing in of the new leafage in the form of a tree or flowers is one, and perhaps the simplest, form of spring festival. It takes little notice of death and winter, uttering and emphasizing only the desire for the joy in life and spring. But in other and severer climates the emotion is fiercer and more complex; it takes the form of a struggle or contest, what the Greeks called an *agon*. Thus on May Day in the Isle of Man a Queen of the May was chosen, and with her twenty maids of honour, together with a troop of young men for escort. But there was not only a Queen of the May, but a Queen of Winter, a man dressed as a woman, loaded with warm clothes and wearing a woollen hood and fur tippet. Winter, too, had attendants like the Queen of the May. The two troops met and fought; and whichever Queen was taken prisoner had to pay the expenses of the feast.

In the Isle of Man the real gist of the ceremony is quite forgotten, it has become a mere play. But among the Esquimaux [1]

[1] Resumed from Dr. Frazer, *Golden Bough*,[2] II, p. 104.

there is still carried on a similar rite, and its magical intent is clearly understood. In autumn, when the storms begin and the long and dismal Arctic winter is at hand, the central Esquimaux divide themselves into two parties called the Ptarmigans and the Ducks. The ptarmigans are the people born in winter, the ducks those born in summer. They stretch out a long rope of sealskin. The ducks take hold of one end, the ptarmigans of the other, then comes a tug-of-war. If the ducks win there will be fine weather through the winter; if the ptarmigans, bad. This autumn festival might, of course, with equal magical intent be performed in the spring, but probably autumn is chosen because, with the dread of the Arctic ice and snow upon them, the fear of winter is stronger than the hope of spring.

The intense emotion towards the weather, which breaks out into these magical *agones*, or " contests," is not very easy to realize. The weather to us now-a-days for the most part damps a day's pleasuring or raises the price of fruit and vegetables. But our main supplies come to us from other lands and other weathers, and we find it hard to think

ourselves back into the state when a bad
harvest meant starvation. The intensely
practical attitude of man towards the seasons,
the way that many of these magical dramatic
ceremonies rose straight out of the emotion
towards the food-supply, would perhaps never
have been fully realized but for the study of
the food-producing ceremonies of the Central
Australians.

The Central Australian spring is not the
shift from winter to summer, from cold to
heat, but from a long, arid, and barren season
to a season short and often irregular in
recurrence of torrential rain and sudden
fertility. The dry steppes of Central Australia
are the scene of a marvellous transformation.
In the dry season all is hot and desolate, the
ground has only patches of wiry scrub, with
an occasional parched acacia tree, all is stones
and sand; there is no sign of animal life save
for the thousand ant-hills. Then suddenly the
rainy season sets in. Torrents fill the rivers,
and the sandy plain is a sheet of water.
Almost as suddenly the rain ceases, the
streams dry up, sucked in by the thirsty ground,
and as though literally by magic a luxuriant
vegetation bursts forth, the desert blossoms

as a rose. Insects, lizards, frogs, birds, chirp, frisk and chatter. No plant or animal can live unless it live quickly. The struggle for existence is keen and short.

It seems as though the change came and life was born by magic, and the primitive Australian takes care that magic should not be wanting, and magic of the most instructive kind. As soon as the season of fertility approaches he begins his rites with the avowed object of making and multiplying the plants, and chiefly the animals, by which he lives; he paints the figure of the emu on the sand with vermilion drawn from his own blood; he puts on emu feathers and gazes about him vacantly in stupid fashion like an emu bird; he makes a structure of boughs like the chrysalis of a Witchetty grub—his favourite food, and drags his body through it in pantomime, gliding and shuffling to promote its birth. Here, difficult and intricate though the ceremonies are, and uncertain in meaning as many of the details must probably always remain, the main emotional gist is clear. It is not that the Australian wonders at and admires the miracle of his spring, the bursting of the flowers and the singing of birds; it is not

that his heart goes out in gratitude to an
All-Father who is the Giver of all good things;
it is that, obedient to the push of life within
him, his impulse is towards food. He must
eat that he and his tribe may grow and
multiply. It is this, his will to live, that he
utters and represents.

The savage utters his will to live, his intense
desire for food; but it should be noted, it is
desire and will and longing, not certainty and
satisfaction that he utters. In this respect
it is interesting to note that his rites and
ceremonies, when periodic, are of fairly long
periods. Winter and summer are not the
only natural periodic cycles; there is the
cycle of day and night, and yet among primitive peoples but little ritual centres round
day and night. The reason is simple. The
cycle of day and night is so short, it recurs
so frequently, that man naturally counted
upon it and had no cause to be anxious. The
emotional tension necessary to ritual was
absent. A few peoples, *e. g.* the Egyptians,
have practised daily incantations to bring
back the sun. Probably they had at first
felt a real tension of anxiety, and then—being

a people hidebound by custom—had gone
on from mere conservatism.   Where the sun
returns at a longer interval, and is even,
as among the Esquimaux, hidden for the long
space of six months, ritual inevitably arises.
They play at cat's-cradle to catch the ball of
the sun lest it should sink and be lost for ever.

Round the moon, whose cycle is long, but
not too long, ritual very early centred, but
probably only when its supposed influence on
vegetation was first surmised.   The moon, as it
were, practises magic herself; she waxes and
wanes, and with her, man thinks, all the vegetable kingdom waxes and wanes too, all but
the lawless onion.   The moon, Plutarch [1] tells
us, is fertile in its light and contains moisture, it
is kindly to the young of animals and to the
new shoots of plants.   Even Bacon [2] held that
observations of the moon with a view to plant-
ing and sowing and the grafting of trees were
" not altogether frivolous."   It cannot too
often be remembered that primitive man has
but little, if any, interest in sun and moon
and heavenly bodies for their inherent beauty
or wonder; he cares for them, he holds them

[1] *De Is. et Os.*, p. 367.
[2] *De Aug. Scient.*, III, 4.

sacred, he performs rites in relation to them mainly when he notes that they bring the seasons, and he cares for the seasons mainly because they bring him food. A season is to him as a *Hora* was at first to the Greeks, *the fruits of a season*, what our farmers would call " a good *year*."

The sun, then, had no ritual till it was seen that he led in the seasons; but long before that was known, it was seen that the seasons were annual, that they went round in a *ring;* and because that annual ring was long in revolving, great was man's hope and fear in the winter, great his relief and joy in the spring. It was literally a matter of death and life, and it was as death and life that he sometimes represented it, as we have seen in the figures of Adonis and Osiris.

Adonis and Osiris have their modern parallels, who leave us in no doubt as to the meaning of their figures. Thus on the 1st of March in Thüringen a ceremony is performed called " Driving out the Death." The young people make up a figure of straw, dress it in old clothes, carry it out and throw it into the river. Then they come back, tell

the good news to the village, and are given
eggs and food as a reward.   In Bohemia the
children carry out a straw puppet and burn
it.   While they are burning it they sing—

"Now carry we Death out of the village,
   The new Summer into the village,
   Welcome, dear Summer,
   Green little corn."

In other parts of Bohemia the song varies;
it is not Summer that comes back but Life.

" We have carried away Death,
   And brought back Life."

In both these cases it is interesting to
note that though Death is dramatically
carried out, the coming back of Life is only
announced, not enacted.

Often, and it would seem quite naturally,
the puppet representing Death or Winter is
reviled and roughly handled, or pelted with
stones, and treated in some way as a sort of
scapegoat.   But in not a few cases, and these
are of special interest, it seems to be the seat
of a sort of magical potency which can be and
is transferred to the figure of Summer or
Life, thus causing, as it were, a sort of Resur-

rection. In Lusatia the women only carry out the Death. They are dressed in black themselves as mourners, but the puppet of straw which they dress up as the Death wears a white shirt. They carry it to the village boundary, followed by boys throwing stones, and there tear it to pieces. Then they cut down a tree and dress it in the white shirt of the Death and carry it home singing.

So at the Feast of the Ascension in Transylvania. After morning service the girls of the village dress up the Death; they tie a threshed-out sheaf of corn into a rough copy of a head and body, and stick a broomstick through the body for arms. Then they dress the figure up in the ordinary holiday clothes of a peasant girl—a red hood, silver brooches, and ribbons galore. They put the Death at an open window that all the people when they go to vespers may see it. Vespers over, two girls take the Death by the arms and walk in front; the rest follow. They sing an ordinary church hymn. Having wound through the village they go to another house, shut out the boys, strip the Death of its clothes, and throw the straw body out of the window to the boys, who fling it into a river. Then one of the girls is dressed in the Death's discarded clothes, and the procession again winds through the village. The same hymn is sung. Thus it is clear that the girl is a sort of resuscitated Death. This resurrection aspect, this passing of the old into the new, will be seen to be of great ritual importance when we come to Dionysos and the Dithyramb.

These ceremonies of Death and Life are more complex than the simple carrying in of green boughs or even the dancing round maypoles. When we have these figures, these " impersonations," we are getting away from the merely emotional dance, from the domain of simple psychological motor discharge to something that is very like rude art, at all events to personification. On this question of personification, in which so much of art and religion has its roots, it is all-important to be clear.

In discussions on such primitive rites as " Carrying out the Death," " Bringing in Summer," we are often told that the puppet of the girl is carried round, buried, burnt; brought back, because it " personifies the Spirit of Vegetation," or it " embodies the

Spirit of Summer." The Spirit of Vegetation is "incarnate in the puppet." We are led, by this way of speaking, to suppose that the savage or the villager first forms an idea or conception of a Spirit of Vegetation and then later "embodies" it. We naturally wonder that he should perform a mental act so high and difficult as abstraction.

A very little consideration shows that he performs at first no abstraction at all; abstraction is foreign to his mental habit. He begins with a vague excited dance to relieve his emotion. That dance has, probably almost from the first, a leader; the dancers choose an actual *person*, and he is the root and ground of *personification*. There is nothing mysterious about the process; the leader does not "embody" a previously conceived idea, rather he begets it. From his personality springs the personification. The abstract idea arises from the only thing it possibly can arise from, the concrete fact. Without *per*ception there is no *con*ception. We noted in speaking of dances (p. 43) how the dance got generalized; how from many commemorations of actual hunts and battles there arose the hunt dance and the war dance. So, from many actual living personal May Queens and Deaths, from many actual men and women decked with leaves, or trees dressed up as men and women, arises *the* Tree Spirit, *the* Vegetation Spirit, *the* Death.

At the back, then, of the fact of personification lies the fact that the emotion is felt collectively, the rite is performed by a band or chorus who dance together *with a common leader*. Round that leader the emotion centres. When there is an act of Carrying-out or Bringing-in he either is himself the puppet or he carries it. Emotion is of the whole band; drama—doing—tends to focus on the leader. This leader, this focus, is then remembered, thought of, imaged; from being *per*ceived year by year, he is finally *con*ceived; but his basis is always in actual fact of which he is but the reflection.

Had there been no periodic festivals, personification might long have halted. But it is easy to see that a recurrent *per*ception helps to form a permanent abstract *con*ception. The different actual recurrent May Kings and " Deaths," *because they recur,* get a sort of permanent life of their own and become beings apart. In this way a conception, a kind of *daimon*, or spirit, is fashioned, who dies and lives again in a perpetual cycle. The periodic festival begets a kind of not immortal, but perennial, god.

Yet the faculty of conception is but dim and feeble in the mind even of the peasant to-day; his function is to perceive the actual fact year by year, and to feel about it. Perhaps a simple instance best makes this clear. The Greek Church does not gladly suffer images in the round, though she delights in picture-images, *eikons*. But at her great spring festival of Easter she makes, in the remote villages, concession to a strong, perhaps imperative, popular need; she allows an image, an actual idol, of the dead Christ to be laid in the tomb that it may rise again. A traveller in Eubœa [1] during Holy Week had been struck by the genuine grief shown at the Good Friday services. On Easter Eve there was the same general gloom and despondency, and he asked an old woman why it was. She answered: "Of course I am anxious; for if Christ does not rise to-morrow, we shall have no corn this year."

[1] J. C. Lawson, *Modern Greek Folk-lore and Ancient Religion*, p. 573.

The old woman's state of mind is fairly
clear.   Her emotion is the old emotion, not
sorrow for the Christ the Son of Mary, but
fear, imminent fear for the failure of food.
The Christ again is not the historical Christ
of Judæa, still less the incarnation of the
Godhead proceeding from the Father; he is
the actual figure fashioned by his village
chorus and laid by the priests, the leaders of
that chorus, in the local sepulchre.

So far, then, we have seen that the vague
emotional dance tends to become a periodic
rite, performed at regular intervals.   The
periodic rite may occur at any date of importance to the food-supply of the community,
in summer, in winter, at the coming of the
annual rains, or the regular rising of a river.
Among Mediterranean peoples, both in ancient
days and at the present time, the Spring
Festival arrests attention.   Having learnt the
general characteristics of this Spring Festival,
we have now to turn to one particular case,
the Spring Festival of the Greeks.   This is all-
important to us because, as will be seen, from
the ritual of this and kindred festivals arose, we
believe, a great form of Art, the Greek drama.

CHAPTER IV

THE tragedies of Æschylus, Sophocles, and Euripides were performed at Athens at a festival known as the Great Dionysia. This took place early in April, so that the time itself makes us suspect that its ceremonies were connected with the spring. But we have more certain evidence. Aristotle, in his treatise on the Art of Poetry, raises the question of the origin of the drama. He was not specially interested in primitive ritual; beast dances and spring mummeries might even have seemed to him mere savagery, the lowest form of " imitation;" but he divined that a structure so complex as Greek tragedy must have arisen out of a simpler form; he saw, or felt, in fact, that art had in some way risen out of ritual, and he has left us a memorable statement.

In describing the " Carrying-out of Summer" we saw that the element of real *drama*, real

75

impersonation, began with the leaders of the
band, with the Queen of the May, and with the
"Death" or the "Winter." Great is our delight
when we find that for Greek drama Aristotle [1]
divined a like beginning. He says:

"Tragedy—as also Comedy—was at first
mere improvisation—the one (tragedy) *origin-
ated with the leaders of the Dithyramb*."

The further question faces us: What was
the Dithyramb? We shall find to our joy that
this obscure-sounding Dithyramb, though before Aristotle's time it had taken literary form,
was in origin a festival closely akin to those
we have just been discussing. The Dithyramb was, to begin with, a spring ritual; and
when Aristotle tells us tragedy arose out of the
Dithyramb, he gives us, though perhaps half
unconsciously, a clear instance of a splendid
art that arose from the simplest of rites;
he plants our theory of the connection of art
with ritual firmly with its feet on historical
ground.

When we use the word "dithyrambic" we
certainly do not ordinarily think of spring.

[1] *Poetics*, IV, 12.

We say a style is " dithyrambic " when it is unmeasured, too ornate, impassioned, flowery. The Greeks themselves had forgotten that the word *Dithyramb* meant a leaping, inspired dance. But they had not forgotten on what occasion that dance was danced. Pindar wrote a Dithyramb for the Dionysiac festival at Athens, and his song is full of springtime and flowers. He bids all the gods come to Athens to dance flower-crowned.

" Look upon the dance, Olympians; send us the grace of Victory, ye gods who come to the heart of our city, where many feet are treading and incense steams : in sacred Athens come to the holy centre-stone. Take your portion of garlands pansy-twined, libations poured from the culling of spring. . . .

" Come hither to the god with ivy bound. Bromios we mortals name Him, and Him of the mighty Voice. . . . The clear signs of his Fulfilment are not hidden, whensoever the chamber of the purple-robed Hours is opened, and nectarous flowers lead in the fragrant spring. Then, then, are flung over the immortal Earth, lovely petals of pansies, and roses are amid our hair; and voices of song

are loud among the pipes, the dancing-floors
are loud with the calling of crowned Semele."

Bromios, " He of the loud cry," is a title of
Dionysos.   Semele is his mother, the Earth;
we keep her name in Nova *Zembla,* "New
Earth."   The song might have been sung at
a " Carrying-in of Summer."   The Horæ,
the Seasons, a chorus of maidens, lead in the
figure of Spring, the Queen of the May, and
they call to Mother Earth to wake, to rise up
from the earth, flower-crowned.

You may *bring back* the life of the Spring
in the form of a tree or a maiden, or you may
summon her to rise from the sleeping Earth.
In Greek mythology we are most familiar with
the Rising-up form.   Persephone, the daughter
of Demeter, is carried below the Earth, and
rises up again year by year.   On Greek vase-
paintings [1] the scene occurs again and again.
A mound of earth is represented,   sometimes
surmounted by a tree; out of the mound a
woman's figure rises; and all about the mound
are figures of dancing dæmons waiting to
welcome her.

[1] See my *Themis,* p. 419.   (1912.)

All this is not mere late poetry and art. It is the primitive art and poetry that come straight out of ritual, out of actual "things done," *dromena*. In the village of Megara, near Athens, the very place where to-day on Easter Tuesday the hills are covered with throngs of dancing men, and specially women, Pausanias [1] saw near the City Hearth a rock called "*Anaklethra*, ' Place of Calling-up,' because, if any one will believe it, when she was wandering in search of her daughter, Demeter called her up there"; and he adds: "The women to this day perform rites analogous to the story told."

These rites of " Calling-up " must have been spring rites, in which, in some pantomimic dance, the uprising of the Earth Spirit was enacted.

Another festival of Uprising is perhaps more primitive and instructive, because it is near akin to the " Carrying out of Winter," and also because it shows clearly the close connection of these rites with the food-supply. Plutarch [2] tells us of a festival held every nine years at Delphi. It was called from the name of the puppet used *Charila*, a word

[1] I, 43. 2.   [2] *Quaest. Græc.* XII.

which originally meant Spring-Maiden, and
is connected with the Russian word *yaro*,
"Spring," and is also akin to the Greek
Charis, "grace," in the sense of increase,
"Give us all *grace*." The rites of *Charila*,
the Gracious One, the Spring-Maiden, were
as follows :

" The king presided and made a distribution
in public of grain and pulse to all, both citizens
and strangers. And the child-image of *Charila*
is brought in. When they had all received
their share, the king struck the image with
his sandal, the leader of the Thyiades lifted
the image and took it away to a precipitous
place, and there tied a rope round the neck
of the image and buried it."

Mr. Calderon has shown that very similar
rites go on to-day in Bulgaria in honour of
Yarilo, the Spring God.

The image is beaten, insulted, let down into
some cleft or cave. It is clearly a " Carrying
out the Death," though we do not know the
exact date at which it was celebrated. It had
its sequel in another festival at Delphi called
Herois, or the " Heroine." Plutarch [1] says it

[1] *Op. cit.*

was too mystical and secret to describe, but he lets us know the main gist.

" Most of the ceremonies of the *Herois* have a mystical reason which is known to the Thyiades, but from the rites that are done in public, one may conjecture it to be a ' Bringing up of Semele.' "

Some one or something, a real woman, or more likely the buried puppet *Charila*, the Spring-Maiden, was brought up from the ground to enact and magically induce the coming of Spring.

These ceremonies of beating, driving out, burying, have all, with the Greeks, as with the savage and the modern peasant, but one real object : to get rid of the season that is bad for food, to bring in and revive the new supply. This comes out very clearly in a ceremony that went on down to Plutarch's time, and he tells us [1] it was " ancestral." It was called " the Driving out of Ox-hunger." By Ox-hunger was meant any great ravenous hunger, and the very intensity and monstrosity of the word takes us back to days when

[1] *Quæst. Symp.*, 693 f.

famine was a grim reality. When Plutarch was *archon* he had, as chief official, to perform the ceremony at the Prytaneion, or Common Hearth. A slave was taken, beaten with rods of a magical plant, and driven out of doors to the words : " Out with Ox-hunger ! In with Wealth and Health ! " Here we see the actual sensation, or emotion, of ravenous hunger gets a name, and thereby a personality, though a less completely abstracted one than Death or Summer. We do not know that the ceremony of Driving out Ox-hunger was performed in the spring, it is only instanced here because, more plainly even than the Charila, when the king distributes pulse and peas, it shows the relation of ancient mimic ritual to food-supply.

If we keep clearly in mind the *object* rather than the exact *date* of the Spring Song we shall avoid many difficulties. A Dithyramb was sung at Delphi through the winter months, which at first seems odd. But we must remember that among agricultural peoples the performance of magical ceremonies to promote fertility and the food supply may begin at any moment after the earth is ploughed and the seed sown. The sowing of the seed is its death and burial; "that which thou sowest is not quickened except it die." When the death and burial are once accomplished the hope of resurrection and new birth begins, and with the hope the magical ceremonies that may help to fulfil that hope. The Sun is new-born in midwinter, at the solstice, and our " New " year follows, yet it is in the spring that, to this day, we keep our great resurrection festival.

We return to our argument, holding steadily in our minds this connection. The Dithyramb is a Spring Song at a Spring Festival, and the importance of the Spring Festival is that it magically promotes the food-supply.

Do we know any more about the Dithyramb? Happily yes, and the next point is as curious as significant.

Pindar, in one of his Odes, asks a strange question :

" Whence did appear the Graces of Dionysos,
    With the Bull-driving Dithyramb ? "

Scholars have broken their own heads and one another's to find a meaning and an answer to the odd query. It is only quite

lately that they have come at all to see that
the Dithyramb was a Spring Song, a primitive
rite. Formerly it was considered to be a
rather elaborate form of lyric poetry invented
comparatively late. But, even allowing it
is the Spring Song, are we much further?
Why should the Dithyramb be bull-driving?
How can driving a Bull help the spring to
come? And, above all, what are the " slender-
ankled " Graces doing, helping to drive the
great unwieldy Bull?

The difficulty about the Graces, or Charites,
as the Greeks called them, is soon settled.
They are the Seasons, or "Hours," and the
chief Season, or Hour, was Spring herself.
They are called Charites, or Graces, because
they are, in the words of the Collect, the
" Givers of all grace," that is, of all increase
physical and spiritual.   But why do they want
to come driving in a Bull?   It is easy to see
why the Givers of all grace lead the Dithyramb, the Spring Song; their coming, with
their " fruits in due season " is the very gist
of the Dithyramb; but why is the Dithyramb
" bull-driving "? Is this a mere " poetical "
epithet? If it is, it is not particularly
poetical.

But Pindar is not, we now know, merely being " poetical," which amounts, according to some scholars, to meaning anything or nothing. He is describing, alluding to, an actual rite or *dromenon* in which a Bull is summoned and driven to come in spring. About that we must be clear. Plutarch, the first anthropologist, wrote a little treatise called *Greek Questions*, in which he tells us all the strange out-of-the-way rites and customs he saw in Greece, and then asks himself what they meant. In his 36th *Question* he asks: " Why do the women of Elis summon Dionysos in their hymns to be present with them with his bull-foot? " And then, by a piece of luck that almost makes one's heart stand still, he gives us the very words of the little ritual hymn the women sang, our earliest " Bull-driving " Spring Song:

" In Spring-time,[1] O Dionysos,
    To thy holy temple come;
To Elis with thy Graces,
    Rushing with thy bull-foot, come,
    Noble Bull, Noble Bull."

[1] The words " in Spring-time " depend on an emendation to me convincing. See my *Themis*, p. 205, note 1.

It is a strange primitive picture—the holy women standing in springtime in front of the temple, summoning the Bull; and the Bull, garlanded and filleted, rushing towards them, driven by the Graces, probably three real women, three Queens of the May, wreathed and flower-bedecked. But what does it mean?

Plutarch tries to answer his own question, and half, in a dim, confused fashion, succeeds. " Is it," he suggests, " that some entitle the god as ' Born of a Bull ' and as a ' Bull ' himself ? . . . or is it that many hold the god is the beginner of sowing and ploughing? " We have seen how a kind of *daimon*, or spirit, of Winter or Summer arose from an actual tree or maid or man disguised year by year as a tree. Did the god Dionysos take his rise in like fashion from the driving and summoning year by year of some holy Bull?

First, we must notice that it was not only at Elis that a holy Bull appears at the Spring Festival. Plutarch asks another instructive *Question* :[1] " Who among the Delphians is the Sanctifier ? " And we find to our amazement that the sanctifier is a Bull. A Bull

[1] IX.

who not only is holy himself, but is so holy that he has power to make others holy, he is the Sanctifier; and, most important for us, he sanctifies by his death in the month Bysios, the month that fell, Plutarch tells us, "at the beginning of spring, the time of the blossoming of many plants."

We do not hear that the "Sanctifier" at Delphi was "driven," but in all probability he was led from house to house, that every one might partake in the sanctity that simply exuded from him. At Magnesia,[1] a city of Asia Minor, we have more particulars. There, at the annual fair year by year the stewards of the city bought a Bull, "the finest that could be got," and at the new moon of the month at the beginning of seedtime they dedicated it, for the city's welfare. The Bull's sanctified life began with the opening of the agricultural year, whether with the spring or the autumn ploughing we do not know. The dedication of the Bull was a high solemnity. He was led in procession, at the head of which went the chief priest and priestess of the city. With them went a herald and the sacrificer, and two bands of youths and

[1] See my *Themis*, p. 151.

maidens. So holy was the Bull that nothing
unlucky might come near him; the youths
and maidens must have both their parents
alive, they must not have been under the
taboo, the infection, of death. The herald
pronounced aloud a prayer for " the safety
of the city and the land, and the citizens,
and the women and children, for peace and
wealth, and for the bringing forth of grain
and of all the other fruits, and of cattle."
All this longing for fertility, for food and
children, focuses round the holy Bull, whose
holiness is his strength and fruitfulness.

The Bull thus solemnly set apart, charged
as it were with the luck of the whole people,
is fed at the public cost. The official charged
with his keep has to drive him into the
market-place, and " it is good for those corn-
merchants who give the Bull grain as a gift,"
good for them because they are feeding,
nurturing, the luck of the State, which is
their own luck. So through autumn and
winter the Bull lives on, but early in April
the end comes. Again a great procession is
led forth, the senate and the priests walk in
it, and with them come representatives of
each class of the State—children and young

boys, and youths just come to manhood, *epheboi*, as the Greeks called them. The Bull is sacrificed, and why? Why must a thing so holy die? Why not live out the term of his life? He dies because he *is* so holy, that he may give his holiness, his strength, his life, just at the moment it is holiest, to his people.

" When they shall have sacrificed the Bull, let them divide it up among those who took part in the procession."

The mandate is clear. The procession included representatives of the whole State. The holy flesh is not offered to a god, it is eaten—to every man his portion—by each and every citizen, that he may get his share of the strength of the Bull, of the luck of the State.

Now at Magnesia, after the holy civic communion, the meal shared, we hear no more. Next year a fresh Bull will be chosen, and the cycle begin again. But at Athens at the annual " Ox-murder," the *Bouphonia*, as it was called, the scene did not so close. The ox was slain with all solemnity, and all

those present partook of the flesh, and then
—the hide was stuffed with straw and sewed
up, and next the stuffed animal was set on
its feet and yoked to a plough as though it
were ploughing. The Death is followed by
a Resurrection. Now this is all-important.
We are so accustomed to think of sacrifice as
the death, the giving up, the renouncing of
something. But *sacrifice* does not mean
" death " at all. It means making holy,
sanctifying; and holiness was to primitive
man just special strength and life. What
they wanted from the Bull was just that
special life and strength which all the year
long they had put into him, and nourished
and fostered. That life was in his blood.
They could not eat that flesh nor drink that
blood unless they killed him. So he must die.
But it was not to give him up to the gods that
they killed him, not to " sacrifice " him in our
sense, but to have him, keep him, eat him, live
by him and through him, by his grace.

And so this killing of the sacred beast was
always a terrible thing, a thing they fain would
have shirked. They fled away after the deed,
not looking backwards; they publicly tried
and condemned the axe that struck the blow.

But their best hope, their strongest desire, was that he had not, could not, really have died. So this intense desire uttered itself in the *dromenon* of his resurrection. If he did not rise again, how could they plough and sow again next year? He must live again, he should, he *did*.

The Athenians were a little ashamed of their " Ox-murder," with its grotesque pantomime of the stuffed, resurrected beast. Just so some of us now-a-days are getting a little shy of deliberately cursing our neighbours on Ash Wednesday. They probably did not feel very keenly about their food-supply, they thought their daily dinner was secure. Anyhow the emotion that had issued in the pantomime was dead, though from sheer habit the pantomime went on. Probably some of the less educated among them thought there " might be something in it," and anyhow it was " as well to be on the safe side." The queer ceremony had got associated with the worship of Olympian Zeus, and with him you must reckon. Then perhaps your brother-in-law was the Ox-striker, and anyhow it was desirable that the women should go; some of the well-born girls had to act as water-carriers.

The Ox-murder was obsolete at Athens, but the spirit of the rite is alive to-day among the Ainos in the remote island of Saghalien. Among the Ainos the Bear is what psychologists rather oddly call the main " food focus," the chief " value centre." And well he may be. Bear's flesh is the Ainos' staple food; they eat it both fresh and salted; bearskins are their principal clothing; part of their taxes are paid in bear's fat. The Aino men spend the autumn, winter and spring in hunting the Bear. Yet we are told the Ainos " worship the Bear "; they apply to it the name *Kamui*, which has been translated god; but it is a word applied to all strangers, and so only means what catches attention, and hence is formidable. In the religion of the Ainos " the Bear plays a chief part," says one writer. The Bear " receives idolatrous veneration," says another. They " worship it after their fashion," says a third. Have we another case of " the heathen in his blindness " ? Only here he " bows down " not to " gods of wood and stone," but to a live thing, uncouth, shambling but gracious—a Bear.

Instead of theorizing as to what the Aino thinks and imagines, let us observe his *doings,* his *dromena*, his rites; and most of all his great spring and autumn rite, the *dromenon* of the Bear. We shall find that, detail for detail, it strangely resembles the Greek *dromenon* of the Bull.

As winter draws to a close among the Ainos, a young Bear is trapped and brought into the village. At first an Aino woman suckles him at her breast, then later he is fed on his favourite food, fish—his tastes are semi-polar. When he is at his full strength, that is, when he threatens to break the cage in which he lives, the feast is held. This is usually in September, or October, that is when the season of bear-hunting begins.

Before the feast begins the Ainos apologize profusely, saying that they have been good to the Bear, they can feed him no longer, they must kill him. Then the man who gives the Bear-feast invites his relations and friends, and if the community be small nearly the whole village attends. On the occasion described by Dr. Scheube about thirty Ainos were present, men, women, and children, all dressed in their best clothes. The woman of the house who had suckled the Bear sat by herself, sad and silent, only now and then she burst into helpless tears. The ceremony began with libations made to the fire-god and to the house-god set up in a corner of the house. Next the master and some of the guests left the hut and offered libations in front of the Bear's cage. A few drops were presented to him in a saucer, which he promptly upset. Then the women and girls danced round the cage, rising and hopping on their toes, and as they danced they clapped their hands and chanted a monotonous chant. The mother and some of the old women cried as they danced and stretched out their arms to the Bear, calling him loving names. The young women who had nursed no Bears laughed, after the manner of the young. The Bear began to get upset, and rushed round his cage, howling lamentably.

Next came a ceremony of special significance which is never omitted at the sacrifice of a Bear. Libations were offered to the *inabos*, sacred wands which stand outside the Aino hut. These wands are about two feet high and are whittled at the top into spiral shavings. *Five new wands with bamboo leaves attached to them* are set up for the festival; the leaves according to the Ainos mean *that the Bear may come to life again.* These wands are specially interesting. The chief focus of attention is of course the Bear, because his flesh is for the Aino his staple food. But vegetation is not quite forgotten. The animal life of the Bear and the vegetable life of the bamboo-leaves are thought of together.

Then comes the actual sacrifice. The Bear is led out of his cage, a rope is thrown round his neck, and he is perambulated round the neighbourhood of the hut. We do not hear that among the Ainos he goes in procession round the village, but among the Gilyaks, not far away in Eastern Siberia, the Bear is led about the villages, and it is held to be specially important that he should be dragged down to the river, for this will ensure the village a plentiful supply of fish. He is then, among the Gilyaks, taken to each hut in the village, and fish, brandy, and other delicacies are offered to him. Some of the people prostrate themselves in front of him and his coming into a house brings a blessing, and if he snuffs at the food, that brings a blessing too.

To return to the Aino Bear. While he is being led about the hut the men, headed by a chief, shoot at the Bear with arrows tipped

with buttons.   But the object of the shooting
is not to kill, only apparently to irritate him.
He is killed at last without shedding of his
sacred blood, and we hope without much pain.
He is taken in front of the sacred wands, a
stick placed in his mouth, and nine men
press his neck against a beam; he dies without
a sound. Meantime the women and girls,
who stand behind the men, dance, lament, and
beat the men who are killing their Bear.
The body of the dead Bear is then laid on a
mat before the sacred wands. A sword and
quiver, taken from the wands, are hung about
the Bear. If it is a She-Bear it is also bedecked with a necklace and rings. Food and
drink, millet broth and millet cakes are
offered to it. It is decked as an Aino, it is
fed as an Aino. It is clear that the Bear is
in some sense a human Bear, an Aino. The
men sit down on mats in front of the Bear and
offer libations, and themselves drink deep.

Now that the death is fairly over the
mourning ends, and all is feasting and merri-
ment. Even the old women lament no more.
Cakes of millet are scrambled for. The bear
is skinned and disembowelled, the trunk is
severed from the head, to which the skin is

left hanging. The blood, which might not be shed before, is now carefully collected in cups and eagerly drunk by the men, for the blood is the life. The liver is cut up and eaten raw. The flesh and the rest of the vitals are kept for the day next but one, when it is divided among all persons present at the feast. It is what the Greeks call a *dais*, a meal divided or distributed. While the Bear is being dismembered the girls dance, in front of the sacred wands, and the old women again lament. The Bear's brain is extracted from his head and eaten, and the skull, severed from the skin, is hung on a pole near the sacred wands. Thus it would seem the life and strength of the bear is brought near to the living growth of the leaves. The stick with which the Bear was gagged is also hung on the pole, and with it the sword and quiver he had worn after his death. The whole congregation, men and women, dance about this strange maypole, and a great drinking bout, in which all men and women alike join, ends the feast.

The rite varies as to detail in different places. Among the Gilyaks the Bear is dressed after death in full Gilyak costume and seated on a bench of honour. In one part the bones and skull are carried out by the oldest people to a place in the forest not far from the village. There all the bones except the skull are buried. After that a young tree is felled a few inches above the ground, its stump is cleft, and the skull wedged into the cleft. When the grass grows over the spot the skull disappears and there is an end of the Bear. Sometimes the Bear's flesh is eaten in special vessels prepared for this festival and only used at it. These vessels, which include bowls, platters, spoons, are elaborately carved with figures of bears and other devices.

Through all varieties in detail the main intent is the same, and it is identical with that of the rite of the holy Bull in Greece and the maypole of our forefathers. Great is the sanctity of the Bear or the Bull or the Tree; the Bear for a hunting people; the Bull for nomads, later for agriculturists; the Tree for a forest folk. On the Bear and the Bull and the Tree are focussed the desire of the whole people. Bear and Bull and Tree are sacred, that is, set apart, because full of a special life and strength intensely desired. They are led and carried about from house to house that their sanctity may touch all, and avail for all; the animal dies that he may be eaten; the Tree is torn to pieces that all may have a fragment; and, above all, Bear and Bull and Tree die only that they may live again.

We have seen (p. 71) that, out of the puppet or the May Queen, actually *per*ceived year after year there arose a remembrance, a mental image, an imagined Tree Spirit, or " Summer," or Death, a thing never actually seen but *con*-ceived. Just so with the Bull. Year by year in the various villages of Greece was seen an actual holy Bull, and bit by bit from the remembrance of these various holy Bulls, who only died to live again each year, there arose the image of a Bull-Spirit, or Bull-Daimon, and finally, if we like to call him so, a Bull-God. The growth of this idea, this *con*ception, must have been much helped by the fact that in some places the dancers attendant on the holy Bull dressed up as bulls and cows. The women worshippers of Dionysos, we are told, wore bulls' horns in imitation of the god, for they represented him in pictures as having a bull's head. *We*

know that a man does not turn into a bull,
or a bull into a man, the line of demarcation
is clearly drawn; but the rustic has no such
conviction even to-day. That crone, his aged
aunt, may any day come in at the window
in the shape of a black cat; why should she
not ? It is not, then, that a god 'takes upon
him the form of a bull,' or is 'incarnate in a
bull,' but that the real Bull and the worshipper
dressed as a bull are seen and remembered
and give rise to an imagined Bull-God; but,
it should be observed, only among gifted,
imaginative, that is, image-making, peoples.
The Ainos have their actual holy Bear, as the
Greeks had their holy Bull; but with them
out of the succession of holy Bears there arises,
alas ! no Bear-God.

We have dwelt long on the Bull-driving
Dithyramb, because it was not obvious on
the face of it how driving a bull could help
the coming of spring. We understand now
why, on the day before the tragedies were performed at Athens, the young men (*epheboi*)
brought in not only the human figure of the
god, but also a Bull " worthy " of the God.
We understand, too, why in addition to the

tragedies performed at the great festival, Dithyrambs were also sung—" Bull-driving Dithyrambs."

We come next to a third aspect of the Dithyramb, and one perhaps the most important of all for the understanding of art, and especially the drama. *The Dithyramb was the Song and Dance of the New Birth.*

Plato is discussing various sorts of odes or songs. " Some," he says, " are prayers to the gods—these are called *hymns ;* others of an opposite sort might best be called *dirges ;* another sort are *pæans,* and another —the birth of Dionysos, I suppose—is called *Dithyramb.*" Plato is not much interested in Dithyrambs. To him they are just a particular kind of choral song; it is doubtful if he even knew that they were Spring Songs; but this he did know, though he throws out the information carelessly—the Dithyramb had for its proper subject the birth or coming to be, the *genesis* of Dionysos.

The common usage of Greek poetry bears out Plato's statement. When a poet is going to describe the birth of Dionysos he calls the god by the title *Dithyrambos.* Thus

an inscribed hymn found at Delphi [1] opens
thus :

" Come, O Dithyrambos, Bacchos, come.

   .   .   .   .

Bromios, come, and coming with thee bring
Holy hours of thine own holy spring.

   .   .   .   .   .   .

All the stars danced for joy. Mirth
Of mortals hailed thee, Bacchos, at thy
    birth."

The Dithyramb is the song of the birth, and
the birth of Dionysos is in the spring, the
time of the maypole, the time of the holy
Bull.

And now we come to a curious thing. We
have seen how a spirit, a dæmon, and perhaps
ultimately a god, develops out of an actual
rite. Dionysos the Tree-God, the Spirit of
Vegetation, is but a maypole once *per*ceived,
then remembered and *con*ceived. Dionysos,
the Bull-God, is but the actual holy Bull
himself, or rather the succession of annual
holy Bulls once perceived, then remembered,

[1] See my *Prolegomena*, p. 439.

generalized, conceived. But the god conceived will surely always be made in the image, the mental image, of the fact perceived. If, then, we have a song and dance of the *birth* of Dionysos, shall we not, as in the Christian religion, have a child-god, a holy babe, a Saviour in the manger; at first in original form as a calf, then as a human child? Now it is quite true that in Greek religion there is a babe Dionysos called *Liknites*, "Him of the Cradle."[1] The rite of waking up, or bringing to light, the child Liknites was performed each year at Delphi by the holy women.

But it is equally clear and certain that *the* Dionysos of Greek worship and of the drama was not a babe in the cradle. He was a goodly youth in the first bloom of manhood, with the down upon his cheek, the time when, Homer says, "youth is most gracious." This is the Dionysos that we know in statuary, the fair, dreamy youth sunk in reverie; this is the Dionysos whom Pentheus despised and insulted because of his young beauty like a woman's. But how could such a Dionysos arise out of a rite of birth? He could not, and he did not. The Dithyramb is also the song

[1] *Prolegomena*, p. 402.

of the second or new birth, the Dithyrambos is the twice-born.

This the Greeks themselves knew. By a false etymology they explained the word *Dithyrambos* as meaning " He of the double door," their word *thyra* being the same as our *door*. They were quite mistaken; *Dithyrambos*, modern philology tells us, is the Divine Leaper, Dancer, and Lifegiver. But their false etymology is important to us, because it shows that they believed the Dithyrambos was the twice-born. Dionysos was born, they fabled, once of his mother, like all men, once of his father's thigh, like no man.

But if the Dithyrambos, the young Dionysos, like the Bull-God, the Tree-God, arises from a *dromenon*, a rite, what is the rite of second birth from which it arises ?

We look in vain among our village customs. If ever rite of second birth existed, it is dead and buried. We turn to anthropology for help, and find this, the rite of the second birth, widespread, universal, over half the savage world.

With the savage, to be twice born is the rule, not the exception. By his first birth he comes into the world, by his second he is born into his tribe. At his first birth he belongs to his mother and the women-folk; at his second he becomes a full-fledged man and passes into the society of the warriors of his tribe. This second birth is a little difficult for us to realize. A boy with us passes very gradually from childhood to manhood, there is no definite moment when he suddenly emerges as a man. Little by little as his education advances he is admitted to the social privileges of the circle in which he is born. He goes to school, enters a workshop or a university, and finally adopts a trade or a profession. In the case of girls, in whose up-bringing primitive savagery is apt to linger, there is still, in certain social strata a ceremony known as Coming Out. A girl's dress is suddenly lengthened, her hair is put up, she is allowed to wear jewels, she kisses her sovereign's hand, a dance is given in her honour; abruptly, from her seclusion in the cocoon state of the schoolroom, she emerges full-blown into society. But the custom, with its half-realized savagery, is already dying, and with boys it does not obtain at all. Both sexes share, of course, the religious rite of Confirmation.

To avoid harsh distinctions, to bridge over abrupt transitions, is always a mark of advancing civilization; but the savage, in his ignorance and fear, lamentably over-stresses distinctions and transitions. The long process of education, of passing from child to man, is with him condensed into a few days, weeks, or sometimes months of tremendous educational emphasis—of what is called "initiation," "going in," that is, entering the tribe. The ceremonies vary, but the gist is always substantially the same. The boy is to put away childish things, and become a grown and competent tribesman. Above all he is to cease to be a woman-thing and become a man. His initiation prepares him for his two chief functions as a tribesman —to be a warrior, to be a father. That to the savage is the main if not the whole Duty of Man.

This "initiation" is of tremendous impor-tance, and we should expect, what in fact we find, that all this emotion that centres about it issues in *dromena*, "rites done." These rites are very various, but they all point one moral, that the former things are passed away and that the new-born man has entered on a new life.

Simplest perhaps of all, and most instructive, is the rite practised by the Kikuyu of British East Africa,[1] who require that every boy, just before circumcision, must be born again. " The mother stands up with the boy crouching at her feet; she pretends to go through all the labour pains, and the boy on being reborn cries like a babe and is washed."

More often the new birth is simulated, or imagined, as a death and a resurrection, either of the boys themselves or of some one else in their presence. Thus at initiation among some tribes of South-east Australia,[2] when the boys are assembled an old man dressed in stringy bark fibre lies down in a grave. He is covered up lightly with sticks and earth, and the grave is smoothed over. The buried man holds in his hand a small bush which seems to be growing from the ground, and other bushes are stuck in the ground round about. The novices are then brought to the edge of the grave and a song is sung. Gradually, as the song goes on, the bush held by the buried man begins to quiver. It moves more and

[1] Frazer, *Totemism and Exogamy*, Vol. I, p. 228.
[2] *The Golden Bough,*[2] III, 424.

more and bit by bit the man himself starts
up from the grave.

The Fijians have a drastic and repulsive
way of simulating death. The boys are
shown a row of seemingly dead men, their
bodies covered with blood and entrails, which
are really those of a dead pig. The first gives
a sudden yell. Up start the men, and then
run to the river to cleanse themselves.

Here the death is vicarious. Another goes
through the simulated death that the initiated
boy may have new life. But often the
mimicry is practised on the boys themselves.
Thus in West Ceram [1] boys at puberty are
admitted to the Kakian association. The
boys are taken blindfold, followed by their
relations, to an oblong wooden shed under the
darkest trees in the depths of the forest.
When all are assembled the high priest calls
aloud on the devils, and immediately a
hideous uproar is heard from the shed. It is
really made by men in the shed with bamboo
trumpets, but the women and children think
it is the devils. Then the priest enters the
shed with the boys, one at a time. A dull
thud of chopping is heard, a fearful cry rings

[1] *The Golden Bough,*[2] III, 442.

out, and a sword dripping with blood is thrust out through the roof. This is the token that the boy's head has been cut off, and that the devil has taken him away to the other world, whence he will return born again. In a day or two the men who act as sponsors to the boys return daubed with mud, and in a half-fainting state like messengers from another world. They bring the good news that the devil has restored the boys to life. The boys themselves appear, but when they return they totter as they walk; they go into the house backwards. If food is given them they upset the plate. They sit dumb and only make signs. The sponsors have to teach them the simplest daily acts as though they were new-born children. At the end of twenty to thirty days, during which their mothers and sisters may not comb their hair, the high priest takes them to a lonely place in the forest and cuts off a lock of hair from the crown of each of their heads. At the close of these rites the boys are men and may marry.

Sometimes the new birth is not simulated but merely suggested. A new name is given, a new language taught, a new dress worn, new dances are danced. Almost always it is accompanied by moral teaching. Thus in the Kakian ceremony already described the boys have to sit in a row cross-legged, without moving a muscle, with their hands stretched out. The chief takes a trumpet, and placing the mouth of it on the hand of each lad, he speaks through it in strange tones, imitating the voice of spirits. He warns the boys on pain of death to observe the rules of the society, and never to reveal what they have seen in the Kakian house. The priests also instruct the boys on their duty to their blood relations, and teach them the secrets of the tribe.

Sometimes it is not clear whether the new birth is merely suggested or represented in pantomime. Thus among the Binbinga of North Australia it is generally believed that at initiation a monstrous being called Kata-jalina, like the Kronos of the Greeks, swallows the boys and brings them up again initiated; but whether there is or is not a *dromenon* or rite of swallowing we are not told.

In totemistic societies, and in the animal secret societies that seem to grow out of them, the novice is born again as the sacred animal

Thus among the Carrier Indians [1] when a man wants to become a *Lulem*, or Bear, however cold the season, he tears off his clothes, puts on a bearskin and dashes into the woods, where he will stay for three or four days. Every night his fellow-villagers will go out in search parties to find him. They cry out *Yi ! Kelulem* ("Come on, Bear ") and he answers with angry growls. Usually they fail to find him, but he comes back at last himself. He is met and conducted to the ceremonial lodge, and there, in company with the rest of the Bears, dances solemnly his first appearance. Disappearance and re-appearance is as common a rite in initiation as simulated killing and resurrection, and has the same object. Both are rites of transition, of passing from one state to another. It has often been remarked, by students of ancient Greek and other ceremonies, that the rites of birth, marriage, and death, which seem to us so different, are to primitive man oddly similar. This is explained if we see that in intent they *are* all the same, all a passing from one social state to another. There are but two factors in every rite, the putting off

[1] *The Golden Bough,*[2] III, p. 438.

of the old, the putting on of the new; you carry out Winter or Death, you bring in Summer or Life. Between them is a midway state when you are neither here nor there, you are secluded, under a *taboo*.

To the Greeks and to many primitive peoples the rites of birth, marriage, and death were for the most part family rites needing little or no social emphasis. But *the* rite which concerned the whole tribe, the essence of which was entrance into the tribe, was the rite of initiation at puberty. This all-important fact is oddly and significantly enshrined in the Greek language. The general Greek word for rite was *tĕlĕtē*. It was applied to all mysteries, and sometimes to marriages and funerals. But it has nothing to do with death. It comes from a root meaning " to grow up." The word *tĕlĕtē* means *rite of growing up*, becoming complete. It meant at first maturity, then rite of maturity, then by a natural extension any rite of initiation that was mysterious. The rites of puberty were in their essence mysterious, because they consisted in initiation into the sanctities of the tribe, the things which society sanctioned and protected, excluding the uninitiated, whether they were young boys, women, or members of other tribes. Then, by contagion, the mystery notion spread to other rites.

We understand now who and what was the god who arose out of the rite, the *dromenon* of tribal initiation, the rite of the new, the second birth. He was Dionysos. His name, according to recent philology, tells us—Dionysos, " Divine Young Man."

When once we see that out of the emotion of the rite and the facts of the rite arises that remembrance and shadow of the rite, that *image* which is the god, we realize instantly that the god of the spring rite *must* be a young god, and in primitive societies, where young women are but of secondary account, he will necessarily be a young *man*. Where emotion centres round tribal initiation he will be a young man just initiated, what the Greeks called a *kouros*, or *ephebos*, a youth of quite different social status from a mere *pais* or boy. Such a youth survives in our King of the May and Jack-in-the Green. Old men and women are for death and winter, the young for life and spring, and most of all the young man or bear or bull or tree just come to maturity.

And because life is one at the Spring Festival, the young man carries a blossoming branch bound with wool of the young sheep. At Athens in spring and autumn alike " they carry out the *Eiresione*, a branch of olive wound about with wool . . . and laden with all sorts of firstfruits, *that scarcity may cease*, and they sing over it:

> " Eiresione brings
> Figs and fat cakes,
> And a pot of honey and oil to mix,
> And a wine-cup strong and deep,
> That she may drink and sleep."

The Eiresione had another name that told its own tale. It was called *Korythalia*,[1] " Branch of blooming youth." The young men, says a Greek orator, are " the Spring of the people."

The excavations of Crete have given to us an ancient inscribed hymn, a Dithyramb, we may safely call it, that is at once a spring-song and a young man-song. The god here

[1] See my *Themis*, p. 503.

invoked is what the Greeks call a *kouros*, a young man. It is sung and danced by young warriors :

" Ho ! Kouros, most Great, I give thee hail, Lord of all that is wet and gleaming; thou art come at the head of thy Daimones. To Diktè for the Year, Oh, march and rejoice in the dance and song."

The leader of the band of *kouroi*, of young men, the real actual leader, has become by remembrance and abstraction, as we noted, a daimon, or spirit, at the head of a band of spirits, and he brings in the new year at spring. The real leader, the " first kouros " as the Greeks called him, is there in the body, but from the succession of leaders year by year they have imaged a spirit leader greatest of all. He is " lord of all that is wet and gleaming," for the May bough, we remember, is drenched with dew and water that it may burgeon and blossom. Then they chant the tale of how of old a child was taken away from its mother, taken by armed men to be initiated, armed men dancing their tribal dance. The stone is unhappily broken here, but enough remains to make the meaning clear.

And because this boy grew up and was initiated into manhood:

" The Horæ (Seasons) began to be fruitful year by year and Dikè to possess mankind, and all wild living things were held about by wealth-loving Peace."

We know the Seasons, the fruit and food bringers, but Dikè is strange. We translate the word " Justice," but Dikè means, not Justice as between man and man, but the order of the world, the *way* of life. It is through this way, this order, that the seasons go round. As long as the seasons observe this order there is fruitfulness and peace. If once that order were overstepped then would be disorder, strife, confusion, barrenness. And next comes a mandate, strange to our modern ears:

" To us also leap for full jars, and leap for fleecy flocks, and leap for fields of fruit and for hives to bring increase."

And yet not strange if we remember the Macedonian farmer (p. 82), who throws his spade into the air that the wheat may be tall, or the Russian peasant girls who leap high in the air crying, " Flax, grow." The leaping of the youths of the Cretan hymn is just the utterance of their tense desire. They have grown up, and with them all live things must grow. By their magic year by year the fruits of the earth come to their annual new birth. And that there be no mistake they end:

" Leap for our cities, and leap for our sea-borne ships, *and for our young citizens*, and for goodly Themis."

They are now young citizens of a fencèd city instead of young tribesmen of the bush, but their magic is the same, and the strength that holds them together is the bond of social custom, social structure, " goodly Themis." No man liveth to himself.

Crete is not Athens, but at Athens in the theatre of Dionysos, if the priest of Dionysos, seated at the great Spring Festival in his beautiful carved central seat, looked across the orchestra, he would see facing him a stone frieze on which was sculptured the Cretan ritual, the armed dancing youths and the child to be year by year reborn.

We have seen what the Dithyramb, from which sprang the Drama, was. A Spring song, a song of Bull-driving, a song and dance of Second Birth; but all this seems, perhaps, not to bring us nearer to Greek drama, rather to put us farther away. What have the Spring and the Bull and the Birth Rite to do with the stately tragedies we know — with Agamemnon and Iphigenia and Orestes and Hippolytos? That is the question before us, and the answer will lead us to the very heart of our subject. So far we have seen that ritual arose from the presentation and emphasis of emotion—emotion felt mainly about food. We have further seen that ritual develops out of and by means of periodic festivals. One of the chief periodic festivals at Athens was the Spring Festival of the Dithyramb. Out of this Dithyramb arose, Aristotle says, tragedy—that is, out of Ritual arose Art. How and Why? That is the question before us.

CHAPTER V

PROBABLY most people when they go to a
Greek play for the first time think it a strange
performance. According, perhaps, more to
their temperament than to their training,
they are either very much excited or very
much bored. In many minds there will be
left a feeling that, whether they have enjoyed
the play or not, they are puzzled : there are
odd effects, conventions, suggestions.

For example, the main deed of the Tragedy,
the slaying of hero or heroine, is not done
on the stage. That disappoints some modern
minds unconsciously avid of realism to the
point of horror. Instead of a fine thrilling
murder or suicide before his very eyes, the
spectator is put off with an account of the
murder done off the stage. This account is
regularly given, and usually at considerable

length, in a " messenger's speech." The messenger's speech is a regular item in a Greek
play, and though actually it gives scope not
only for fine elocution, but for real dramatic
effect, in theory we feel it undramatic, and
a modern actor has sometimes much ado to
make it acceptable. The spectator is told
that all these, to him, odd conventions are
due to Greek restraint, moderation, good
taste, and yet for all their supposed restraint
and reserve, he finds when he reads his Homer
that Greek heroes frequently burst into floods
of tears when a self-respecting Englishman
would have suffered in silence.

Then again, specially if the play be by
Euripides, it ends not with a "curtain,"
not with a great decisive moment, but with
the appearance of a god who says a few lines
of either exhortation or consolation or recon-
ciliation, which, after the strain and stress
of the action itself, strikes some people as
rather stilted and formal, or as rather flat
and somehow unsatisfying. Worse still, there
are in many of the scenes long dialogues, in
which the actors wrangle with each other,
and in which the action does not advance
so quickly as we wish. Or again, instead of

beginning with the action, and having our curiosity excited bit by bit about the plot, at the outset some one comes in and tells us the whole thing in the prologue. Prologues we feel, are out of date, and the Greeks ought to have known better. Or again, of course we admit that tragedy must be tragic, and we are prepared for a decent amount of lamentation, but when an antiphonal lament goes on for pages, we weary and wish that the chorus would stop lamenting and *do* something.

At the back of our modern discontent there is lurking always this queer anomaly of the chorus. We have in our modern theatre no chorus, and when, in the opera, something of the nature of a chorus appears in the ballet, it is a chorus that really dances to amuse and excite us in the intervals of operatic action; it is not a chorus of doddering and pottering old men, moralizing on an action in which they are too feeble to join. Of course if we are classical scholars we do not cavil at the choral songs; the extreme difficulty of scanning and construing them alone commands a traditional respect; but if we are merely modern spectators, we may be re-

spectful, we may even feel strangely excited,
but we are certainly puzzled. The reason of
our bewilderment is simple enough. These
prologues and messengers' speeches and ever-
present choruses that trouble us are ritual
forms still surviving at a time when the *drama*
has fully developed out of the *dromenon*. We
cannot here examine all these ritual forms in
detail;[1] one, however, the chorus, strangest
and most beautiful of all, it is essential we
should understand.

Suppose that these choral songs have been
put into English that in any way represents
the beauty of the Greek; then certainly
there will be some among the spectators who
get a thrill from the chorus quite unknown
to any modern stage effect, a feeling of emotion
heightened yet restrained, a sense of entering
into higher places, filled with a larger and a
purer air—a sense of beauty born clean out
of conflict and disaster.

A suspicion dawns upon the spectator that,
great though the tragedies in themselves are,
they owe their peculiar, their incommunicable
beauty largely to this element of the chorus
which seemed at first so strange.

[1] See Bibliography at end for Professor Murray's
examination.

Now by examining this chorus and understanding its function—nay, more, by considering the actual *orchestra*, the space on which the chorus danced, and the relation of that space to the rest of the theatre, to the stage and the place where the spectators sat—we shall get light at last on our main central problem : How did art arise out of ritual, and what is the relation of both to that actual life from which both art and ritual sprang ?

The dramas of Æschylus certainly, and perhaps also those of Sophocles and Euripides, were played not upon the stage, and not in the *theatre*, but, strange though it sounds to us, in the *orchestra*. The *theatre* to the Greeks was simply " the place of seeing, the place where the spectators sat ; what they called the skēnē or *scene*, was the tent or hut in which the actors dressed. But the kernel and centre of the whole was the *orchestra*, the circular *dancing-place* of the chorus ; and, as the orchestra was the kernel and centre of the theatre, so the chorus, the band of dancing and singing men —this chorus that seems to us so odd and even superfluous—was the centre and kernel and starting-point of the drama. The chorus

danced and sang that Dithyramb we know
so well, and from the leaders of that Dithyramb we remember tragedy arose, and the
chorus were at first, as an ancient writer tells
us, just men and boys, tillers of the earth,
who danced when they rested from sowing
and ploughing.

Now it is in the relation between the
orchestra or dancing-place of the chorus,
and the *theatre* or place of the spectators, a
relation that shifted as time went on, that
we see mirrored the whole development from
ritual to art—from *dromenon* to drama.

The orchestra on which the Dithyramb was
danced was just a circular dancing-place
beaten flat for the convenience of the dancers,
and sometimes edged by a stone basement to
mark the circle. This circular orchestra is
very well seen in the theatre of Epidaurus,
of which a sketch is given in Fig. 1. The
orchestra here is surrounded by a splendid
theatron, or spectator place, with seats rising
tier above tier. If we want to realize the
primitive Greek orchestra or dancing-place,
we must think these stone seats away.
Threshing-floors are used in Greece to-day as

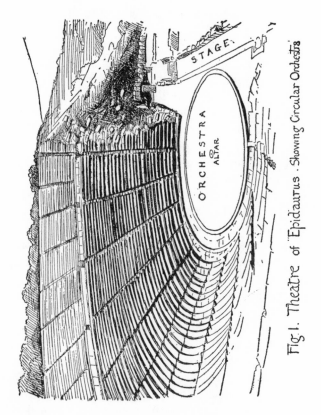

Fig.1. Theatre of Epidaurus. Showing Circular Orchestra

ORCHESTRA
ALTAR

STAGE

convenient dancing-places. The dance tends
to be circular because it is round some sacred
thing, at first a maypole, or the reaped corn,
later the figure of a god or his altar. On this
dancing-place the whole body of worshippers
would gather, just as now-a-days the whole
community will assemble on a village green.
There is no division at first between actors
and spectators; all are actors, all are doing
the thing done, dancing the dance danced.
Thus at initiation ceremonies the whole tribe
assembles, the only spectators are the uninitiated, the women and children. No one
at this early stage thinks of building a *theatre*,
a spectator place. It is in the common act,
the common or collective emotion, that ritual
starts. This must never be forgotten.

The most convenient spot for a mere
dancing-place is some flat place. But any
one who travels through Greece will notice
instantly that all the Greek theatres that
remain at Athens, at Epidaurus, at Delos,
Syracuse, and elsewhere, are built against the
side of hills. None of these are very early;
the earliest ancient orchestra we have is at
Athens. It is a simple stone ring, but it is
built against the steep south side of the

Acropolis. The oldest festival of Dionysos was, as will presently be seen, held in quite another spot, in the *agora*, or market-place. The reason for moving the dance was that the wooden seats that used to be set up on a sort of " grand stand " in the market-place fell down, and it was seen how safely and comfortably the spectators could be seated on the side of a steep hill.

The spectators are a new and different element, the dance is not only danced, but it is watched from a distance, it is a spectacle; whereas in old days all or nearly all were worshippers acting, now many, indeed most, are spectators, watching, feeling, thinking, not doing. It is in this new attitude of the spectator that we touch on the difference between ritual and art; the *dromenon*, the thing actually done by yourself has become a *drama*, a thing also done, but abstracted from your doing. Let us look for a moment at the psychology of the spectator, at his behaviour.

Artists, it is often said, and usually felt, are so unpractical. They are always late for dinner, they forget to post their letters and to return the books or even money that is lent

them.   Art is to most people's minds a sort
of luxury, not a necessity.   In but recently
bygone days music, drawing, and dancing were
no part of a training for ordinary life, they
were taught at school as " accomplishments,"
paid for as " extras."   Poets on their side
equally used to contrast art and life, as though
they were things essentially distinct.

" Art is long, and Time is fleeting."

Now commonplaces such as these, being
unconscious utterances of the collective mind,
usually contain much truth, and are well
worth weighing.   Art, we shall show later,
is profoundly connected with life; it is nowise
superfluous.   But, for all that, art, both its
creation and its enjoyment, is unpractical.
Thanks be to God, life is not limited to the
practical.
    When we say art is unpractical, we mean
that art is *cut loose from immediate action.*
Take a simple instance.   A man—or perhaps
still better a child—sees a plate of cherries.
Through his senses comes the stimulus of the
smell of the cherries, and their bright colour
urging him, luring him to eat.   He eats and
is satisfied; the cycle of normal behaviour is

complete; he is a man or a child of action, but
he is no artist, and no art-lover. Another
man looks at the same plate of cherries. His
sight and his smell lure him and urge him to
eat. He does *not* eat; the cycle is not com-
pleted, and, because he does not eat, the
sight of those cherries, though perhaps not the
smell, is altered, purified from desire, and in
some way intensified, enlarged. If he is just
a man of taste, he will take what we call an
" æsthetic " pleasure in those cherries. If he is
an actual artist, he will paint not the cherries,
but his vision of them, his purified emotion
towards them. He has, so to speak, come out
from the chorus of actors, of cherry-eaters,
and become a spectator.

I borrow, by his kind permission, a beautiful
instance of what he well calls " Psychical
Distance " from the writings of a psychologist.[1]

" Imagine a fog at sea : for most people
it is an experience of acute unpleasantness.
Apart from the physical annoyance and
remoter forms of discomfort, such as delays,
it is apt to produce feelings of peculiar anxiety,
fears of invisible dangers, strains of watching

[1] Mr. Edward Bullough, *The British Journal of Psychology* (1912), p. 88.

and listening for distant and unlocalized signals. The listless movements of the ship and her warning calls soon tell upon the nerves of the passengers; and that special, expectant tacit anxiety and nervousness, always associated with this experience, make a fog the dreaded terror of the sea (all the more terrifying because of its very silence and gentleness) for the expert seafarer no less than the ignorant landsman.

" Nevertheless, a fog at sea can be a source of intense relish and enjoyment. Abstract from the experience of the sea-fog, for the moment, its danger and practical unpleasantness; . . . direct the attention to the features ' objectively ' constituting the phenomena— the veil surrounding you with an opaqueness as of transparent milk, blurring the outlines of things and distorting their shapes into weird grotesqueness; observe the carrying power of the air, producing the impression as if you could touch some far-off siren by merely putting out your hand and letting it lose itself behind that white wall; note the curious creamy smoothness of the water, hypercritically denying as it were, any suggestion of danger; and, above all, the strange solitude and remoteness from the world, as it can be found only on the highest mountain tops; and the experience may acquire, in its uncanny mingling of repose and terror, a flavour of such concentrated poignancy and delight as to contrast sharply with the blind and distempered anxiety of its other aspects. This contrast, often emerging with startling suddenness, is like the momentary switching on of some new current, or the passing ray of a brighter light, illuminating the outlook upon perhaps the most ordinary and familiar objects—an impression which we experience sometimes in instants of direst extremity, when our practical interest snaps like a wire from sheer over-tension, and we watch the consummation of some impending catastrophe with the marvelling unconcern of a mere spectator.''

It has often been noted that two, and two only, of our senses are the channels of art and give us artistic material. These two senses are sight and hearing. Touch and its special modifications, taste and smell, do not go to the making of art. Decadent French novelists, such as Huysmann, make their heroes

revel in perfume-symphonies, but we feel that
the sentiment described is morbid and unreal,
and we feel rightly. Some people speak of a
cook as an "artist," and a pudding as a "perfect
poem," but a healthy instinct rebels. Art,
whether sculpture, painting, drama, music,
is of sight or hearing. The reason is simple.
Sight and hearing are the distant senses;
sight is, as some one has well said, " touch at
a distance." Sight and hearing are of things
already detached and somewhat remote;
they are the fitting channels for art which is
cut loose from immediate action and reaction.
Taste and touch are too intimate, too immediately vital. In Russian, as Tolstoi has
pointed out (and indeed in other languages
the same is observable), the word for beauty
(*krasota*) means, to begin with, only that
which pleases the sight. Even hearing is
excluded. And though latterly people have
begun to speak of an " ugly deed " or of " beautiful music," it is not good Russian. The
simple Russian does not make Plato's divine
muddle between the good and the beautiful.
If a man gives his coat to another, the
Russian peasant, knowing no foreign language,
will not say the man has acted " beautifully."

To see a thing, to feel a thing, as a work of
art, we must, then, become for the time unpractical, must be loosed from the fear and
the flurry of actual living, must become
spectators. Why is this? Why can we not
live and look at once? The *fact* that we
cannot is clear.   If we watch a friend drowning
we do not note the exquisite curve made by
his body as he falls into the water, nor the
play of the sunlight on the ripples as he disappears below the surface; we should be in-
human, æsthetic fiends if we did.   And again,
why?   It would do our friend no harm that
we should enjoy the curves and the sunlight,
provided we also threw him a rope.   But the
simple fact is that we *cannot* look at the curves
and the sunlight because our whole being is
centred on acting, on saving him; we cannot
even, at the moment, fully feel our own terror
and impending loss.   So again if we want to see
and to feel the splendour and vigour of a lion,
or even to watch the cumbrous grace of a
bear, we prefer that a cage should intervene.
The cage cuts off the need for motor actions;
it interposes the needful physical and moral
distance, and we are free for contemplation.
Released from our own terrors, we see more and

better, and we feel differently. A man intent on action is like a horse in blinkers, he goes straight forward, seeing only the road ahead.

Our brain is, indeed, it would seem, in part, an elaborate arrangement for providing these blinkers. If we saw and realized the whole of everything, we should want to do too many things. The brain allows us not only to remember, but, which is quite as important, to forget and neglect; it is an organ of oblivion. By neglecting most of the things we see and hear, we can focus just on those which are important for action; we can cease to be potential artists and become efficient practical human beings; but it is only by limiting our view, by a great renunciation as to the things we see and feel. The artist does just the reverse. He renounces doing in order to practise seeing. He is by nature what Professor Bergson calls " distrait," aloof, absent-minded, intent only, or mainly, on contemplation. That is why the ordinary man often thinks the artist a fool, or, if he does not go so far as that, is made vaguely uncomfortable by him, never really under- stands him. The artist's focus, all his system

of values, is different, his world is a world of
images which are his realities.

The distinction between art and ritual,
which has so long haunted and puzzled us,
now comes out quite clearly, and also in part
the relation of each to actual life. Ritual, we
saw, was a re-presentation or a pre-presen-
tation, a re-doing or pre-doing, a copy or
imitation of life, but,—and this is the important point,—always with a practical end.
Art is also a representation of life and the
emotions of life, but cut loose from immediate
action. Action may be and often is represented, but it is not that it may lead on to a
practical further end. The end of art is in
itself. Its value is not mediate but *immediate*. Thus ritual *makes, as it were, a bridge
between real life and art,* a bridge over which
in primitive times it would seem man must
pass. In his actual life he hunts and fishes
and ploughs and sows, being utterly intent
on the practical end of gaining his food; in
the *dromenon* of the Spring Festival, though
his *acts* are unpractical, being mere singing
and dancing and mimicry, his *intent* is practical, to induce the return of his food-supply.

In the drama the representation may remain
for a time the same, but the intent is altered :
man has come out from action, he is separate
from the dancers, and has become a spectator.
The drama is an end in itself.

We know from tradition that in Athens
ritual became art, a *dromenon* became the
drama, and we have seen that the shift is
symbolized and expressed by the addition of
the *theatre*, or spectator-place, to the orchestra,
or dancing-place.   We have also tried to
analyse the meaning of the shift.   It remains
to ask what was its cause.   Ritual does not
always develop into art, though in all probability dramatic art has always to go through
the stage of ritual.   The leap from real life
to the emotional contemplation of life cut
loose from action would otherwise be too
wide.   Nature abhors a leap, she prefers to
crawl over the ritual bridge.   There seem
at Athens to have been two main causes why
the *dromenon* passed swiftly, inevitably, into
the drama.   They are, first, the decay of
religious faith ; second, the influx from abroad
of a new culture and new dramatic material.
It may seem surprising to some that the

decay of religious faith should be an impulse
to the birth of art. We are accustomed to
talk rather vaguely of art " as the handmaid
of religion "; we think of art as " inspired
by " religion. But the decay of religious
faith of which we now speak is not the decay
of faith in a god, or even the decay of some
high spiritual emotion; it is the decay of a
belief in the efficacy of certain magical rites,
and especially of the Spring Rite. So long
as people believed that by excited dancing,
by bringing in an image or leading in a bull
you could induce the coming of Spring, so
long would the *dromena* of the Dithyramb
be enacted with intense enthusiasm, and with
this enthusiasm would come an actual acces-
sion and invigoration of vital force. But,
once the faintest doubt crept in, once men
began to be guided by experience rather than
custom, the enthusiasm would die down, and
the collective invigoration no longer be felt.
Then some day there will be a bad summer,
things will go all wrong, and the chorus will
sadly ask : " Why should I dance my dance ? "
They will drift away or become mere spectators of a rite established by custom. The
rite itself will die down, or it will live on

only as the May Day rites of to-day, a children's play, or at best a thing done vaguely "for luck."

The spirit of the rite, the belief in its efficacy, dies, but the rite itself, the actual mould, persists, and it is this ancient ritual mould, foreign to our own usage, that strikes us to-day, when a Greek play is revived, as odd and perhaps chill. A *chorus*, a band of dancers there must be, because the drama arose out of a ritual dance. An *agon*, or contest, or wrangling, there will probably be, because Summer contends with Winter, Life with Death, the New Year with the Old. A tragedy must be tragic, must have its *pathos*, because the Winter, the Old Year, must die. There must needs be a swift transition, a clash and change from sorrow to joy, what the Greeks called a *peripeteia*, a *quick-turn-round*, because, though you carry out Winter, you bring in Summer. At the end we shall have an Appearance, an Epiphany of a god, because the whole gist of the ancient ritual was to summon the spirit of life. All these ritual forms haunt and shadow the play, whatever its plot, like ancient traditional ghosts; they underlie and sway the movement and the speeches like some compelling rhythm.

Now this ritual mould, this underlying rhythm, is a fine thing in itself; and, moreover, it was once shaped and cast by a living spirit: the intense immediate desire for food and life, and for the return of the seasons which bring that food and life. But we have seen that, once the faith in man's power magically to bring back these seasons waned, once he began to doubt whether he could really carry out Winter and bring in Summer, his emotion towards these rites would cool. Further, we have seen that these rites repeated year by year ended, among an imaginative people, in the mental creation of some sort of dæmon or god. This dæmon, or god, was more and more held responsible on his own account for the food-supply and the order of the Horæ, or Seasons; so we get the notion that this dæmon or god himself led in the Seasons; Hermes dances at the head of the Charites, or an Eiresione is carried to Helios and the Horæ. The thought then arises that this man-like dæmon who rose from a real King of the May, must himself be approached and dealt with as a man, bargained with, sacrificed to. In a word, in place of *dromena*, things done, we get gods worshipped; in place of sacraments, holy bulls killed and eaten in common, we get sacrifices in the modern sense, holy bulls offered to yet holier gods. The relation of these figures of gods to art we shall consider when we come to sculpture.

So the *dromenon*, the thing done, wanes, the prayer, the praise, the sacrifice waxes. Religion moves away from drama towards theology, but the ritual mould of the *dromenon* is left ready for a new content.

Again, there is another point. The magical *dromenon*, the Carrying out of Winter, the Bringing in of Spring, is doomed to an inherent and deadly monotony. It is only when its magical efficacy is intensely believed that it can go on. The life-history of a holy bull is always the same; its magical essence is that it should be the same. Even when the life-dæmon is human his career is unchequered. He is born, initiated, or born again; he is married, grows old, dies, is buried; and the old, old story is told again next year. There are no fresh personal incidents, peculiar to one particular dæmon. If the drama rose from the Spring Song only, beautiful it might

be, but with a beauty that was monotonous,
a beauty doomed to sterility.

We seem to have come to a sort of *impasse*,
the spirit of the *dromenon* is dead or dying,
the spectators will not stay long to watch a
doing doomed to monotony. The ancient
moulds are there, the old bottles, but where
is the new wine? The pool is stagnant;
what angel will step down to trouble the
waters?

Fortunately we are not left to conjecture
what *might* have happened. In the case of
Greece we know, though not as clearly as we
wish, what did happen. We can see in part
why, though the *dromena* of Adonis and
Osiris, emotional as they were and intensely
picturesque, remained mere ritual; the *dromenon* of Dionysos, his Dithyramb, blossomed
into drama.

Let us look at the facts, and first at some
structural facts in the building of the theatre.

We have seen that the orchestra, with its
dancing chorus, stands for ritual, for the
stage in which all were worshippers, all
joined in a rite of practical intent. We
further saw that the *theatre*, the place for the

spectators, stood for art. In the orchestra
all is life and dancing; the marble *seats* are
the very symbol of rest, aloofness from action,
contemplation. The seats for the spectators
grow and grow in importance till at last they
absorb, as it were, the whole spirit, and give
their name *theatre* to the whole structure;
action is swallowed up in contemplation.
But contemplation of what? At first, of
course, of the ritual dance, but not for long.
That, we have seen, was doomed to a deadly
monotony. In a Greek theatre there was
not only orchestra and a spectator-place,
there was also a *scene* or *stage*.

The Greek word for stage is, as we said,
skenè, our scene. The *scene* was not a stage
in our sense, *i. e.* a platform raised so that
the players might be better viewed. It was
simply a tent, or rude hut, in which the players,
or rather dancers, could put on their ritual
dresses. The fact that the Greek theatre
had, to begin with, no permanent stage in
our sense, shows very clearly how little it
was regarded as a spectacle. The ritual
dance was a *dromenon*, a thing to be done,
not a thing to be looked at. The history of
the Greek stage is one long story of the

encroachment of the stage on the orchestra. At first a rude platform or table is set up, then scenery is added; the movable tent is translated into a stone house or a temple front. This stands at first outside the orchestra; then bit by bit the *scene* encroaches till the sacred circle of the dancing-place is cut clean across. As the drama and the stage wax, the *dromenon* and the orchestra wane.

This shift in the relation of dancing-place and stage is very clearly seen in Fig. 2, a plan of the Dionysiac theatre at Athens (p. 144). The old circular orchestra shows the dominance of ritual; the new curtailed orchestra of Roman times and semicircular shape shows the dominance of the spectacle.

Greek tragedy arose, Aristotle has told us, from the *leaders* of the Dithyramb, the leaders of the Spring Dance. The Spring Dance, the mime of Summer and Winter, had, as we have seen, only one actor, one actor with two parts—Death and Life. With only one play to be played, and that a one-actor play, there was not much need for a stage. A *scene*, that is a *tent*, was needed, as we saw, because all the dancers had to put on their

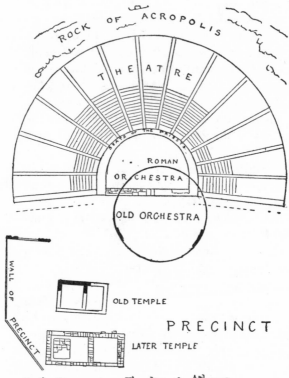

Fig 2 Dionysiac Theatre at Athens.

144

ritual gear, but scarcely a stage. From a rude platform the prologue might be spoken, and on that platform the Epiphany or Appearance of the New Year might take place; but the play played, the life-history of the life-spirit, was all too familiar; there was no need to look, the thing was to dance. You need a stage—not necessarily a raised stage, but a place apart from the dancers—when you have new material for your players, something you need to look at, to attend to. In the sixth century B.C., at Athens, came *the* great innovation. Instead of the old plot, the life-history of the life-spirit, with its deadly monotony, new plots were introduced, not of life-spirits but of human individual heroes. In a word, Homer came to Athens, and out of Homeric stories playwrights began to make their plots. This innovation was the death of ritual monotony and the *dromenon*. It is not so much the old that dies as the new that kills.

Æschylus himself is reported to have said that his tragedies were "slices from the great banquet of Homer." The metaphor is not a very pleasing one, but it expresses a truth.

By Homer, Æschylus meant not only our *Iliad* and *Odyssey*, but the whole body of Epic or Heroic poetry which centred round not only the Siege of Troy but the great expedition of the *Seven Against Thebes*, and which, moreover, contained the stories of the heroes before the siege began, and their adventures after it was ended. It was from these heroic sagas for the most part, though not wholly, that the *myths* or plots of not only Æschylus but also Sophocles and Euripides, and a host of other writers whose plays are lost to us, are taken. The new wine that was poured into the old bottles of the *dromena* at the Spring Festival was the heroic saga. We know as an historical fact, the name of the man who was mainly responsible for this inpouring—the great democratic tyrant Peisistratos. We must look for a moment at what Peisistratos found, and then pass to what he did.

He found an ancient Spring *dromenon*, perhaps well-nigh effete. Without destroying the old he contrived to introduce the new, to add to the old plot of Summer and Winter the life-stories of heroes, and thereby arose the drama.

Let us look first, then, at what Peisistratos found.

The April festival of Dionysos at which the great dramas were performed was not the earliest festival of the god. Thucydides [1] expressly tells us that on the 12th day of the month Anthesterion, that is in the quite early spring, at the turn of our February and March, were celebrated *the more ancient Dionysia*. It was a three-days' festival.[2] On the first day, called " Cask-opening," the jars of new wine were broached. Among the Bœotians the day was called not the day of Dionysos, but the day of the Good or Wealthy Daimon. The next day was called the day of the " Cups "—there was a contest or *agon* of drinking. The last day was called the " Pots," and it, too, had its " Pot-Contests." It is the ceremonies of this day that we must notice a little in detail; for they are very surprising. " Casks," " Cups," and " Pots," sound primitive enough. "Casks" and "Cups" go well with the wine-god, but the " Pots " call for explanation.

The second day of the " Cups," joyful

[1] II, 15.
[2] See my *Themis*, p. 289, and *Prolegomena*, p. 35.

though it sounds, was by the Athenians counted unlucky, because on that day they believed " the ghosts of the dead rose up." The sanctuaries were roped in, each house-holder anointed his door with pitch, that the ghost who tried to enter might catch and stick there. Further, to make assurance doubly sure, from early dawn he chewed a bit of buckthorn, a plant of strong purgative powers, so that, if a ghost should by evil chance go down his throat, it should at least be promptly expelled.

For two, perhaps three, days of constant anxiety and ceaseless precautions the ghosts fluttered about Athens. Men's hearts were full of nameless dread, and, as we shall see, hope. At the close of the third day the ghosts, or, as the Greeks called them, *Keres*, were bidden to go. Some one, we do not know whom, it may be each father of a house-hold, pronounced the words : " Out of the door, ye Keres; it is no longer Anthesteria," and, obedient, the Keres were gone.

But before they went there was a supper for these souls. All the citizens cooked a *pan-spermia* or " Pot-of-all-Seeds," but of this Pot-of-all-Seeds no citizen tasted. It was made

over to the spirits of the under-world and
Hermes their daimon, Hermes " Psycho-
pompos," Conductor, Leader of the dead.

We have seen how a forest people, dependent
on fruit trees and berries for their food, will
carry a maypole and imagine a tree-spirit.
But a people of agriculturists will feel and do
and think quite otherwise; they will look,
not to the forest but to the earth for their
returning life and food; they will sow seeds
and wait for their sprouting, as in the gardens
of Adonis. Adonis seems to have passed
through the two stages of Tree-Spirit and
Seed-Spirit; his effigy was sometimes a tree
cut down, sometimes his planted " Gardens."
Now seeds are many, innumerable, and they
are planted in the earth, and a people who
bury their dead know, or rather feel, that the
earth is dead man's land. So, when they
prepare a pot of seeds on their All Souls' Day,
it is not really or merely as a " supper for
the souls," though it may be that kindly
notion enters. The ghosts have other work
to do than to eat their supper and go. They
take that supper " of all seeds," that *pan-
spermia*, with them down to the world below,

that they may tend it and foster it and bring it back in autumn as a pot of *all fruits*, a *pankarpia.*

" Thou fool, that which thou sowest is not quickened except it die."

The dead, then, as well as the living—this is for us the important point—had their share in the *dromena* of the " more ancient Dionysia." These agricultural spring *dromena* were celebrated just outside the ancient city gates, in the *agora*, or place of assembly, on a circular dancing-place, near to a very primitive sanctuary of Dionysos which was opened only once in the year, at the Feast of Cups. Just outside the gates was celebrated yet another festival of Dionysos equally primitive, called the " Dionysia in the Fields." It had the form though not the date of our May Day festival. Plutarch [1] thus laments over the " good old times ": " In ancient days," he says, " our fathers used to keep the feast of Dionysos in homely, jovial fashion. There was a procession, a jar of wine and a *branch ;* then some one dragged in a goat,

[1] *De Cupid. div.* 8.

another followed bringing a wicker basket
of figs, and, to crown all, the phallos." It
was just a festival of the fruits of the whole
earth : wine and the basket of figs and the
branch for vegetation, the goat for animal
life, the phallos for man. No thought here
of the dead, it is all for the living and his
food.

Such sanctities even a great tyrant might
not tamper with. But if you may not upset
the old you may without irreverence add
the new. Peisistratos probably cared little
for, and believed less in, magical ceremonies
for the renewal of fruits, incantations of the
dead. We can scarcely picture him chewing
buckthorn on the day of the " Cups," or
anointing his front door with pitch to keep
out the ghosts. Very wisely he left the
Anthesteria and the kindred festival " in the
fields" where and as they were. But for his
own purposes he wanted to do honour to
Dionysos, and also above all things to enlarge
and improve the rites done in the god's
honour, so, leaving the old sanctuary to its
fate, he built a new temple on the south side
of the Acropolis where the present theatre

now stands, and consecrated to the god a
new and more splendid precinct.

He did not build the present theatre, we
must always remember that. The rows of
stone seats, the chief priest's splendid marble
chair, were not erected till two centuries later.
What Peisistratos did was to build a small
stone temple (see Fig. 2), and a great round
orchestra of stone close beside it. Small
fragments of the circular foundation can still
be seen. The spectators sat on the hill-side
or on wooden seats; there was as yet no
permanent *theátron* or spectator-place, still
less a stone stage; the *dromena* were done
on the dancing-place. But for spectator-
place they had the south slope of the Acropolis. What kind of wooden stage they had
unhappily we cannot tell. It may be that
only a portion of the orchestra was marked
off.

Why did Peisistratos, if he cared little for
magic and ancestral ghosts, take such trouble
to foster and amplify the worship of this
maypole-spirit, Dionysos? Why did he add
to the Anthesteria, the festival of the family
ghosts and the peasant festival " in the fields,"

a new and splendid festival, a little later in
the spring, the *Great Dionysia*, or *Dionysia
of the City?* One reason among others was
this—Peisistratos was a "tyrant."

Now a Greek "tyrant" was not in our
sense "tyrannical." He took his own way,
it is true, but that way was to help and serve
the common people. The tyrant was usually
raised to his position by the people, and he
stood for democracy, for trade and industry,
as against an idle aristocracy. It was but a
rudimentary democracy, a democratic tyranny,
the power vested in one man, but it stood
for the rights of the many as against the few.
Moreover, Dionysos was always of the people,
of the "working classes," just as the King
and Queen of the May are now. The upper
classes worshipped then, as now, not the Spirit
of Spring but *their own ancestors*. But—
and this was what Peisistratos with great
insight saw—Dionysos must be transplanted
from the fields to the city. The country is
always conservative, the natural stronghold
of a landed aristocracy, with fixed traditions;
the city with its closer contacts and consequent
swifter changes, and, above all, with its ac-
quired, not inherited, wealth, tends towards

democracy. Peisistratos left the Dionysia
" in the fields," but he added the Great
Dionysia " in the city."

Peisistratos was not the only tyrant who
concerned himself with the *dromena* of Dionysos. Herodotos[1] tells the story of another
tyrant, a story which is like a window opening suddenly on a dark room. At Sicyon, a
town near Corinth, there was in the *agora*
a *heroon*, a hero-tomb, of an Argive hero,
Adrastos.

" The Sicyonians," says Herodotos, " paid
other honours to Adrastos, and, moreover,
they celebrated his death and disasters with
tragic choruses, not honouring Dionysos but
Adrastos." We think of " tragic " choruses
as belonging exclusively to the theatre and
Dionysos; so did Herodotus, but clearly here
they belonged to a local hero. His adventures
and his death were commemorated by choral
dances and songs. Now when Cleisthenes
became tyrant of Sicyon he felt that the cult
of the local hero was a danger. What did he
do ? Very adroitly he brought in from Thebes
another hero as rival to Adrastos. He then
split up the worship of Adrastos; part of

[1] V, 66.

his worship, and especially his sacrifices, he gave to the new Theban hero, but the tragic choruses he gave to the common people's god, to Dionysos. Adrastos, the objectionable hero, was left to dwindle and die. No local hero can live on without his cult.

The act of Cleisthenes seems to us a very drastic proceeding. But perhaps it was not really so revolutionary as it seems. The local hero was not so very unlike a local *dæmon*, a Spring or Winter spirit. We have seen in the Anthesteria how the paternal ghosts are expected to look after the seeds in spring. The more important the ghost the more incumbent is this duty upon him. *Noblesse oblige.* On the river Olynthiakos[1] in Northern Greece stood the tomb of the hero Olynthos, who gave the river its name. In the spring months of Anthesterion and Elaphebolion the river rises and an immense shoal of fish pass from the lake of Bolbe to the river of Olynthiakos, and the inhabitants round about can lay in a store of salt fish for all their needs. "And it is a wonderful fact that they never pass by the monument of Olynthus. They say that

[1] *Athen.* VIII, ii, 334 f. See my *Prolegomena*, p. 54.

formerly the people used to perform the accustomed rites to the dead in the month Elaphebolion, but now they do them in Anthesterion, *and that on this account the fish come up in those months only* in which they are wont to do honour to the dead." The river is the chief source of the food-supply, so to send fish, not seeds and flowers, is the dead hero's business.

Peisistratos was not so daring as Cleisthenes. We do not hear that he disturbed or diminished any local cult. He did not attempt to move the Anthesteria with its ghost cult; he only added a new festival, and trusted to its recent splendour gradually to efface the old. And at this new festival he celebrated the deeds of other heroes, not local but of greater splendour and of wider fame. If he did not bring Homer to Athens, he at least gave Homer official recognition. Now to bring Homer to Athens was like opening the eyes of the blind.

Cicero, in speaking of the influence of Peisistratos on literature, says: " He is said to have arranged in their present order the works of Homer, which were previously in confusion." He arranged them not for what we should call " publication," but for public recitation, and another tradition adds that he or his son fixed the order of their recitation at the great festival of " All Athens," the Panathenaia. Homer, of course, was known before in Athens in a scrappy way; now he was publicly, officially promulgated. It is probable, though not certain, that the " Homer " which Peisistratos prescribed for recitation at the Panathenaia was just our *Iliad* and *Odyssey*, and that the rest of the heroic cycle, all the remaining " slices " from the heroic banquet, remained as material for dithyrambs and dramas. The " tyranny " of Peisistratos and his son lasted from 560 to 501 B.C.; tradition said that the first dramatic contest was held in the new theatre built by Peisistratos in 535 B.C., when Thespis won the prize. Æschylus was born in 525 B.C.; his first play, with a plot from the heroic saga, the *Seven Against Thebes*, was produced in 467 B.C. It all came very swiftly, the shift from the dithyramb as Spring Song to the heroic drama was accomplished in something much under a century. Its effect on the whole of Greek life and religion—nay, on the whole of subsequent literature and thought—was incalculable. Let us try to see why.

Homer was the outcome, the expression, of an " heroic " age. When we use the word " heroic " we think vaguely of something brave, brilliant, splendid, something exciting and invigorating. A hero is to us a man of clear, vivid personality, valiant, generous, perhaps hot-tempered, a good friend and a good hater. The word " hero " calls up such figures as Achilles, Patroklos, Hector, figures of passion and adventure. Now such figures, with their special virtues, and perhaps their proper vices, are not confined to Homer. They occur in any and every heroic age. We are beginning now to see that heroic poetry, heroic characters, do not arise from any peculiarity of race or even of geographical surroundings, but, given certain social conditions, they may, and do, appear anywhere and at any time. The world has seen several heroic ages, though it is, perhaps, doubtful if it will ever see another. What, then, are the conditions that produce an heroic age ? and why was this influx of heroic poetry, coming just when it did, of such immense influence on, and importance to, the development of Greek dramatic art? Why had it power to change the old, stiff, ritual dithyramb into the new and living drama? Why, above all things, did the democratic tyrant Peisistratos so eagerly welcome it to Athens?

In the old ritual dance the individual was nothing, the choral band, the group, everything, and in this it did but reflect primitive tribal life. Now in the heroic *saga* the individual is everything, the mass of the people, the tribe, or the group, are but a shadowy background which throws up the brilliant, clear-cut personality into a more vivid light. The epic poet is all taken up with what he called *klea andron*, "glorious deeds of men," of individual heroes; and what these heroes themselves ardently long and pray for is just this glory, this personal distinction, this deathless fame for their great deeds. When the armies meet it is the leaders who fight in single combat. These glorious heroes are for the most part kings, but not kings in the old sense, not hereditary kings bound to the soil and responsible for its fertility. Rather they are leaders in war and adventure; the homage paid them is a personal devotion for personal character; the leader must win his followers by bravery, he must keep them by personal generosity. Moreover, heroic wars are oftenest not tribal feuds consequent on tribal raids, more often they arise from personal grievances, personal jealousies; the siege of Troy is undertaken not because the Trojans have raided the cattle of the Achæans, but because a single Trojan, Paris, has carried off Helen, a single Achæan's wife.

Another noticeable point is that in heroic poems scarcely any one is safely and quietly at home. The heroes are fighting in far-off lands or voyaging by sea; hence we hear little of tribal and even of family ties. The real centre is not the hearth, but the leader's tent or ship. Local ties that bind to particular spots of earth are cut, local differences fall into abeyance, a sort of cosmopolitanism, a forecast of pan-Hellenism, begins to arise. And a curious point—all this is reflected in the gods. We hear scarcely anything of local cults, nothing at all of local magical maypoles and Carryings-out of Winter and Bringings-in of Summer, nothing whatever of " Suppers " for the souls, or even of worship paid to particular local heroes. A man's ghost when he dies does not abide in its grave ready to rise at springtime and help the seeds to sprout; it goes to a remote and shadowy region, a common, pan-Hellenic Hades. And so with the gods themselves; they are cut clean from earth and from the local bits of earth out of which they grew—the sacred trees and holy stones and rivers and still holier beasts. There is not a holy Bull to be found in all Olympus, only figures of men, bright and vivid and intensely personal, like so many glorified, transfigured Homeric heroes.

In a word, the heroic spirit, as seen in heroic poetry, is the outcome of a society cut loose from its roots, of a time of migrations, of the shifting of populations.[1] But more is needed, and just this something more the age that gave birth to Homer had. We know now that before the northern people whom we call Greeks, and who called themselves Hellenes, came down into Greece, there had grown up in the basin of the Ægean a civilization splendid, wealthy, rich in art and already ancient, the civilization that has come to light at Troy, Mycenæ, Tiryns, and most of

[1] Thanks to Mr. H. M. Chadwick's *Heroic Age* (1912).

all in Crete. The adventurers from North and South came upon a land rich in spoils, where a chieftain with a band of hardy followers might sack a city and dower himself and his men with sudden wealth. Such conditions, such a contact of new and old, of settled splendour beset by unbridled adventure, go to the making of a heroic age, its virtues and its vices, its obvious beauty and its hidden ugliness. In settled, social conditions, as has been well remarked, " most of the heroes would sooner or later have found themselves in prison."

A heroic age, happily for society, cannot last long; it has about it while it does last a sheen of passing and pathetic splendour, such as that which lights up the figure of Achilles, but it is bound to fade and pass. A heroic *society* is almost a contradiction in terms. Heroism is for individuals. If a society is to go on at all it must strike its roots deep in some soil, native or alien. The bands of adventurers must disband and go home, or settle anew on the land they have conquered. They must beat their swords into plowshares and their spears into pruning-hooks. Their gallant, glorious leader must become a sober, home-keeping, law-giving and law-abiding king; his followers must abate their individuality and make it subserve a common social purpose.

Athens, in her sheltered peninsula, lay somewhat outside the tide of migrations and heroic exploits. Her population and that of all Attica remained comparatively unchanged; her kings are kings of the stationary, law-abiding, state-reforming type; Cecrops, Erechtheus, Theseus, are not splendid, flashing, all-conquering figures like Achilles and Agamemnon. Athens might, it would seem, but for the coming of Homer, have lain stagnant in a backwater of conservatism, content to go on chanting her traditional Spring Songs year by year. It is a wonderful thing that this city of Athens, beloved of the gods, should have been saved from the storm and stress, sheltered from what might have broken, even shattered her, spared the actual horrors of a heroic *age*, yet given heroic *poetry*, given the clear wine-cup poured when the ferment was over. She drank of it deep and was glad and rose up like a giant refreshed.

We have seen that to make up a heroic age there must be two factors, the new and the old; the young, vigorous, warlike people must seize on, appropriate, in part assimilate, an old and wealthy civilization. It almost seems as if we might go a step farther, and say that for every great movement in art or literature we must have the same conditions, a contact of new and old, of a new spirit seizing or appropriated by an old established order. Anyhow for Athens the historical fact stands certain. The amazing development of the fifth-century drama is just this, the old vessel of the ritual Dithyramb filled to the full with the new wine of the heroic *saga;* and it would seem that it was by the hand of Peisistratos, the great democratic tyrant, that the new wine was outpoured.

Such were roughly the outside conditions under which the drama of art grew out of the *dromena* of ritual. The racial secret of the individual genius of Æschylus and the forgotten men who preceded him we cannot hope to touch. We can only try to see the conditions in which they worked and mark the splendid new material that lay to their hands. Above all things we can see that this material, these Homeric *saga*, were just fitted to give the needed impulse to art. The Homeric *saga* had for an Athenian poet just that remoteness from immediate action which, as we have seen, is the essence of art as contrasted with ritual.

Tradition says that the Athenians fined the dramatic poet Phrynichus for choosing as the plot of one of his tragedies the Taking of Miletus. Probably the fine was inflicted for political party reasons, and had nothing whatever to do with the question of whether the subject was " artistic " or not. But the story may stand, and indeed was later understood to be, a sort of allegory as to the attitude of art towards life. To understand and still more to contemplate life you must come out from the choral dance of life and stand apart. In the case of one's own sorrows, be they national or personal, this is all but impossible. We can ritualize our sorrows, but not turn them into tragedies. We cannot stand back far enough to see the picture; we want to be doing, or at least lamenting. In the case of the sorrows of others this standing back is all too easy. We not only bear their pain with easy stoicism, but we picture it dispassionately at a safe distance; we feel *about* rather than *with* it. The trouble is that we do not feel enough. Such was the attitude of the Athenian towards the doings and sufferings of Homeric heroes. They stood towards them as spectators. These heroes had not the intimate sanctity of home-grown things, but they had sufficient traditional sanctity to make them acceptable as the material of drama.

Adequately sacred though they were, they were yet free and flexible. It is impiety to alter the myth of your local hero, it is impossible to recast the myth of your local dæmon—that is fixed forever—his conflict, his *agon,* his death, his *pathos,* his Resurrection and its heralding, his Epiphany. But the stories of Agamemnon and Achilles, though at home these heroes were local *daimones,* have already been variously told in their wanderings from place to place, and you can mould them more or less to your will. Moreover, these figures are already personal and individual, not representative puppets, mere functionaries like the May Queen and Winter; they have life-histories of their own, never quite to be repeated. It is in this blend of the individual and the general, the personal and the universal, that one element at least of all really great art will be found to lie; and just here at Athens we get a glimpse of the moment of fusion; we see a definite historical reason why and how the universal in *dromena* came to include the particular in drama. We see, moreover, how in place of the old monotonous plots, intimately connected with actual practical needs, we get material cut off from immediate reactions, seen as it were at the right distance, remote yet not too remote. We see, in a word, how a ritual enacted year by year became a work of art that was a " possession for ever."

Possibly in the mind of the reader there may have been for some time a growing discomfort, an inarticulate protest. All this about *dromena* and drama and dithyrambs, bears and bulls, May Queens and Tree-Spirits, even about Homeric heroes, is all very well, curious and perhaps even in a way interesting, but it is not at all what he expected, still less what he wants. When he bought a book with the odd incongruous title, *Ancient Art and Ritual*, he was prepared to put up with some remarks on the artistic side of ritual, but he did expect to be told something about what the ordinary man calls art, that is, statues and pictures. Greek drama is no doubt a form of ancient art, but acting is not to the reader's mind the chief of arts. Nay, more, he has heard doubts raised lately—and he shares them—as to whether acting and dancing, about which so much has been said, are properly speaking arts at all. Now about painting and sculpture there is no doubt. Let us come to business.

To a business so beautiful and pleasant as Greek sculpture we shall gladly come, but a word must first be said to explain the reason of our long delay. The main contention of the present book is that ritual and art have, in emotion towards life, a common root, and further, that primitive art develops normally, at least in the case of the drama, straight out of ritual. The nature of that primitive ritual from which the drama arose is not very familiar to English readers. It has been necessary to stress its characteristics. Almost everywhere, all over the world, it is found that primitive ritual consists, not in prayer and praise and sacrifice, but in mimetic dancing. But it is in Greece, and perhaps Greece only, in the religion of Dionysos, that we can actually trace, if dimly, the transition steps that led from dance to drama, from ritual to art. It was, therefore, of the first importance to realize the nature of the dithyramb from which the drama rose, and so far as might be to mark the cause and circumstances of the transition.

Leaving the drama, we come in the next chapter to Sculpture; and here, too, we shall see how closely art was shadowed by that ritual out of which she sprang.

CHAPTER VI

GREEK SCULPTURE : THE PANATHENAIC
FRIEZE AND THE APOLLO BELVEDERE

In passing from the drama to Sculpture we
make a great leap. We pass from the living
thing, the dance or the play acted by real
people, the thing *done*, whether as ritual or
art, whether *dromenon* or *drama*, to the thing
made, cast in outside material rigid form, a
thing that can be looked at again and again,
but the making of which can never actually
be re-lived whether by artist or spectator.

Moreover, we come to a clear threefold distinction and division hitherto neglected. We
must at last sharply differentiate the artist,
the work of art, and the spectator. The artist
may, and usually indeed does, become the
spectator of his own work, but the spectator
is not the artist. The work of art is, once
executed, forever distinct both from artist
and spectator. In the primitive choral dance
all three—artist, work of art, spectator—were

fused, or rather not yet differentiated. Handbooks on art are apt to begin with the discussion of rude decorative patterns, and after leading up through sculpture and painting, something vague is said at the end about the primitiveness of the ritual dance. But historically and also genetically or logically the dance in its inchoateness, its undifferentiatedness, comes first. It has in it a larger element of emotion, and less of presentation. It is this inchoateness, this undifferentiatedness, that, apart from historical fact, makes us feel sure that logically the dance is primitive.

To illustrate the meaning of Greek sculpture and show its close affinity with ritual, we shall take two instances, perhaps the best-known of those that survive, one of them in relief, the other in the round, the Panathenaic frieze of the Parthenon at Athens and the Apollo Belvedere, and we shall take them in chronological order. As the actual frieze and the statue cannot be before us, we shall discuss no technical questions of style or treatment, but simply ask how they came to be, what human need do they express. The Parthenon frieze is in the British Museum, the Apollo

Belvedere is in the Vatican at Rome, but is readily accessible in casts or photographs. The outlines given in Figs. 5 and 6 can of course only serve to recall subject-matter and design.

The Panathenaic frieze once decorated the *cella* or innermost shrine of the Parthenon, the temple of the Maiden Goddess Athena. It twined like a ribbon round the brow of the building and thence it was torn by Lord Elgin and brought home to the British Museum as a national trophy, for the price of a few hundred pounds of coffee and yards of scarlet cloth. To realize its meaning we must always think it back into its place. Inside the *cella*, or shrine, dwelt the goddess herself, her great image in gold and ivory; outside the shrine was sculptured her worship by the whole of her people. For the frieze is nothing but a great ritual procession translated into stone, the Panathenaic procession, or procession of *all* the Athenians, of all Athens, in honour of the goddess who was but the city incarnate, Athena.

" A wonder enthroned on the hills and the sea,
A maiden crowned with a fourfold glory,

That none from the pride of her head may
    rend;
Violet and olive leaf, purple and hoary,
Song-wreath and story the fairest of fame,
Flowers that the winter can blast not nor
    bend,
A light upon earth as the sun's own flame,
A name as his name—
Athens, a praise without end."

                Swinburne : *Erechtheus*, 141.

Sculptural Art, at least in this instance,
comes out of ritual, has ritual as its subject,
is embodied ritual. The reader perhaps at
this point may suspect that he is being juggled
with, that, out of the thousands of Greek
reliefs that remain to us, just this one instance
has been selected to bolster up the writer's
art and ritual theory. He has only to walk
through any museum to be convinced at once
that the author is playing quite fair. Practically the whole of the reliefs that remain to
us from the archaic period, and a very large
proportion of those at later date, when they
do not represent heroic mythology, are ritual
reliefs, " votive " reliefs as we call them; that
is, prayers or praises translated into stone.

Of the choral dance we have heard much, of the procession but little, yet its ritual importance was great. In religion to-day the dance is dead save for the dance of the choristers before the altar at Seville. But the procession lives on, has even taken to itself

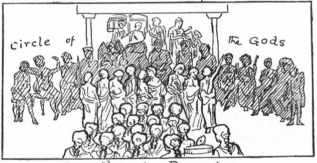

E
Presentation of the Peplos.

circle of   The Gods

Panathenaic Procession.
Fig. 3.

new life. It is a means of bringing masses of people together, of ordering them and co-ordinating them. It is a means for the magical spread of supposed good influence, of " grace." Witness the " Beating of the Bounds" and the frequent processions of the Blessed Sacrament in Roman Catholic lands.

The Queen of the May and the Jack-in-the-Green still go from house to house. Now-a-days it is to collect pence; once it was to

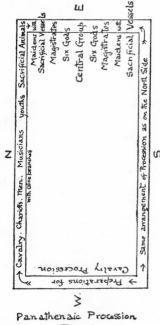

Panathenaic Procession.
FIG. 4.

diffuse " grace " and increase. We remember the procession of the holy Bull at Magnesia and the holy Bear at Saghalien (pp. 92–100).

What, then, was the object of the Pan-athenaic procession? It was first, as its name indicates, a procession that brought all Athens together. Its object was social and political, to express the unity of Athens. Ritual in primitive times is always social, collective.

The arrangement of the procession is shown in Figs. 3 and 4 (pp. 174, 175). In Fig. 3 we see the procession as it were in real life, just as it is about to enter the temple and the presence of the Twelve Gods. These gods are shaded black because in reality invisible. Fig. 4 is a diagram showing the position of the various parts of the procession in the sculptural frieze. At the west end of the temple the procession begins to form : the youths of Athens are mounting their horses. It divides, as it needs must, into two halves, one sculptured on the north, one on the south side of the *cella*. After the throng of the cavalry getting denser and denser we come to the chariots, next the sacrificial animals, sheep and restive cows, then the instruments of sacrifice, flutes and lyres and baskets and trays for offerings; men who carry blossoming olive-boughs; maidens with water-vessels and drinking-cups. The whole tumult of the gathering is marshalled and at last met and, as it were, held in check, by a band of magistrates who face the procession just as it enters the presence of the twelve seated gods, at the east end. The whole body politic of the gods has come down to feast with the whole body politic of Athens and her allies, of whom these gods are but the projection and reflection. The gods are there together because man is collectively assembled.

The great procession culminates in a sacrifice and a communal feast, a sacramental feast like that on the flesh of the holy Bull at Magnesia. The Panathenaia was a high festival including rites and ceremonies of diverse dates, an armed dance of immemorial antiquity that may have dated from the days when Athens was subject to Crete, and a recitation ordered by Peisistratos of the poems of Homer.

Some theorists have seen in art only an extension of the " play instinct," just a liberation of superfluous vitality and energies, as it were a rehearsing for life. This is not our view, but into all art, in so far as it is a cutting off of motor reactions, there certainly enters an element of recreation. It is interesting to note that to the Greek mind religion was specially connected with the notion rather of a festival than a fast. Thucydides[1] is assuredly by nature no reveller, yet religion is to him mainly a "rest from toil." He makes Perikles say: "Moreover, we have provided for our spirit by many opportunities of recreation, by the celebration of games and sacrifices throughout the year." To the anonymous writer known as the "Old Oligarch" the main gist of religion appears to be a decorous social enjoyment. In easy aristocratic fashion he rejoices that religious ceremonials exist to provide for the less well-to-do citizens suitable amusements that they would otherwise lack. "As to sacrifices and sanctuaries and festivals and precincts, the People, knowing that it is impossible for each man individually to sacrifice and feast and have sacrifices and an ample and beautiful city, has discovered by what means he may enjoy these privileges."

In the procession of the Panathenaia all Athens was gathered together, but—and this is important—for a special purpose, more

[1] II, 38.

primitive than any great political or social
union. Happily this purpose is clear; it is
depicted in the central slab of the east end of
the frieze (Fig. 5). A priest is there represented receiving from the hands of a boy a
great *peplos* or robe. It is the sacred robe of
Athena woven for her and embroidered by
young Athenian maidens and offered to her

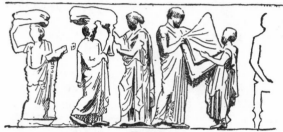

FIG. 5.

every five years. The great gold and ivory
statue in the Parthenon itself had no need of
a robe; she would scarcely have known what
to do with one; her raiment was already of
wrought gold, she carried helmet and spear
and shield. But there was an ancient image
of Athena, an old Madonna of the people,
fashioned before Athena became a warrior
maiden. This image was rudely hewn in
wood, it was dressed and decked doll-fashion

like a May Queen, and to her the great *peplos* was dedicated. The *peplos* was hoisted as a sail on the Panathenaic ship, and this ship Athena had borrowed from Dionysos himself, who went every spring in procession in a ship-car on wheels to open the season for sailing. To a seafaring people like the Athenians the opening of the sailing season was all-important, and naturally began not at midsummer but in spring.

The sacred *peplos*, or robe, takes us back to the old days when the spirit of the year and the " luck " of the people was bound up with a rude image. The life of the year died out each year and had to be renewed. To make a new image was expensive and inconvenient, so, with primitive economy it was decided that the life and luck of the image should be renewed by re-dressing it, by offering to it each year a new robe. We remember (p. 60) how in Thuringia the new puppet wore the shirt of the old and thereby new life was passed from one to the other. But behind the old image we can get to a stage still earlier, when there was at the Panathenaia no image at all, only a yearly maypole; a bough hung with ribbons and

cakes and fruits and the like. A bough was
cut from the sacred olive tree of Athens,
called the *Moria* or Fate Tree. It was bound
about with fillets and hung with fruit and
nuts and, in the festival of the Panathenaia,
they carried it up to the Acropolis to give to
Athena *Polias*, " Her-of-the-City," and as they
went they sang the old Eiresione song (p. 114).
Polias is but the city, the *Polis* incarnate.

This *Moria*, or Fate Tree, was the very
life of Athens; the life of the olive which
fed her and lighted her was the very life of
the city. When the Persian host sacked the
Acropolis they burnt the holy olive, and it
seemed that all was over. But next day it
put forth a new shoot and the people knew
that the city's life still lived. Sophocles[1]
sang of the glory of the wondrous life tree
of Athens :

" The untended, the self-planted, self-defended
        from the foe,
    Sea-gray, children-nurturing olive tree that
        here delights to grow,
    None may take nor touch nor harm it, head-
        strong youth nor age grown bold.

    [1] *Oed. Col.* 694, trans. D. S. MacColl.

For the round of Morian Zeus has been its
  watcher from of old;
He beholds it, and, Athene, thy own sea-
  gray eyes behold."

The holy tree carried in procession is, like
the image of Athena, made of olive-wood,
just the incarnate life of Athens ever
renewed.

The Panathenaia was not, like the Dithyramb, a spring festival. It took place in
July at the height of the summer heat, when
need for rain was the greatest. But the
month Hecatombaion, in which it was celebrated, was the first month of the Athenian
year and the day of the festival was the
birthday of the goddess. When the goddess
became a war-goddess, it was fabled that
she was born in Olympus, and that she sprang
full grown from her father's head in glittering
armour. But she was really born on earth,
and the day of her birth was the birthday
of every earthborn goddess, the day of the
beginning of the new year, with its returning
life. When men observe only the actual
growth of new green life from the ground,
this birthday will be in spring; when they
begin to know that the seasons depend on

the sun, or when the heat of the sun causes
great need of rain, it will be at midsummer,
at the solstice, or in northern regions where
men fear to lose the sun in midwinter, as with
us. The frieze of the Parthenon is, then, but
a primitive festival translated into stone, a
rite frozen to a monument.

Passing over a long space of time we come
to our next illustration, the Apollo Belvedere
(Fig. 6).

It might seem that here at last we have
nothing primitive; here we have art pure
and simple, ideal art utterly cut loose from
ritual, " art for art's sake." Yet in this Apollo
Belvedere, this product of late and accomplished, even decadent art, we shall see most
clearly the intimate relation of art and ritual;
we shall, as it were, walk actually across that
transition bridge of ritual which leads from
actual life to art.

The date of this famous Apollo cannot
be fixed, but it is clearly a copy of a type
belonging to the fourth century B.C. The
poise of the figure is singular and, till its intent
is grasped, unsatisfactory. Apollo is caught in
swift motion but seems, as he stands delicately
poised, to be about to fly rather than to run.

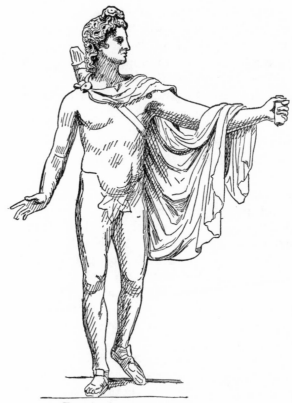

THE APOLLO BELVEDERE
FIG. 6.

184

He stands tiptoe and in a moment will have left the earth. The Greek sculptor's genius was all focussed, as we shall presently see, on the human figure and on the mastery of its many possibilities of movement and action. Greek statues can roughly be dated by the way they stand. At first, in the archaic period, they stand firmly planted with equal weight on either foot, the feet close together. Then one foot is advanced, but the weight still equally divided, an almost impossible position. Next, the weight is thrown on the right foot; and the left knee is bent. This is of all positions the loveliest for the human body. We allow it to women, forbid it to men save to "æsthetes." If the back numbers of *Punch* be examined for the figure of "Postlethwaite" it will be seen that he always stands in this characteristic relaxed pose.

When the sculptor has mastered the possible he bethinks him of the impossible. He will render the human body flying. It may have been the accident of a mythological subject that first suggested the motive. Leochares, a famous artist of the fourth century B.C., made a group of Zeus in the form of an eagle carrying off Ganymede. A replica of the group is preserved in the Vatican, and should stand for comparison near the Apollo. We have the same tiptoe poise, the figure just about to leave the earth. Again, it is not a dance, but a flight. This poise is suggestive to us because it marks an art cut loose, as far as may be, from earth and its realities, even its rituals.

What is it that Apollo is doing? The question and suggested answers have occupied many treatises. There is only one answer: We do not know. It was at first thought that the Apollo had just drawn his bow and shot an arrow. This suggestion was made to account for the pose; but that, as we have seen, is sufficiently explained by the flight-motive. Another possible solution is that Apollo brandishes in his uplifted hand the ægis, or goatskin shield, of Zeus. Another suggestion is that he holds as often a lustral, or laurel bough, that he is figured as Daphnephoros, " Laurel-Bearer."

We do not know if the Belvedere Apollo carried a laurel, but we *do* know that it was of the very essence of the god to be a Laurel-Bearer. That, as we shall see in a moment, he, like Dionysos, arose in part out of a rite, a rite of Laurel-Bearing — a *Daphnephoria.* We have not got clear of ritual yet. When Pausanias,[1] the ancient traveller, whose note-book is our chief source about these early festivals, came to Thebes he saw a hill sacred to Apollo, and after describing the temple on the hill he says :

" The following custom is still, I know, observed at Thebes. A boy of distinguished family and himself well-looking and strong is made the priest of Apollo, *for the space of a year.* The title given him is Laurel-Bearer (Daphnephoros), for these boys wear wreaths made of laurel."

We know for certain now what these yearly priests are : they are the Kings of the Year, the Spirits of the Year, May-Kings, Jacks-o'-the-Green. The name given to the boy is enough to show he carried a laurel branch, though Pausanias only mentions a wreath. Another ancient writer gives us more details.[2] He says in describing the festival of the Laurel-Bearing :

" They wreathe a pole of olive wood with laurel and various flowers. On the top is

[1] IX, 10, 4.   [2] See my *Themis*, p. 438.

fitted a bronze globe from which they suspend smaller ones. Midway round the pole they place a lesser globe, binding it with purple fillets, but the end of the pole is decked with saffron. By the topmost globe they mean the sun, to which they actually compare Apollo. The globe beneath this is the moon; the smaller globes hung on are the stars and constellations, and the fillets are the course of the year, for they make them 365 in number. The Daphnephoria is headed by a boy, both whose parents are alive, and his nearest male relation carries the filleted pole. The Laurel-Bearer himself, who follows next, holds on to the laurel; he has his hair hanging loose, he wears a golden wreath, and he is dressed out in a splendid robe to his feet and he wears light shoes. There follows him a band of maidens holding out boughs before them, to enforce the supplication of the hymns."

This is the most elaborate maypole ceremony that we know of in ancient times. The globes representing sun and moon show us that we have come to a time when men know that the fruits of the earth in due season depended on the heavenly bodies. The year with its 365 days is a Sun-Year. Once this Sun-Year established and we find that the times of the solstices, midwinter and midsummer became as, or even more, important than the spring itself. The date of the *Daphnephoria* is not known.

At Delphi itself, the centre of Apollo-worship, there was a festival called the *Stepteria*, or festival " of those who make the wreathes," in which " mystery " a Christian Bishop, St. Cyprian, tells us he was initiated. In far-off Tempe—that wonderful valley that is still the greenest spot in stony, barren Greece, and where the laurel trees still cluster—there was an altar, and near it a laurel tree. The story went that Apollo had made himself a crown from this very laurel, and *taking in his hand a branch of this same laurel,* i. e. as Laurel-Bearer, had come to Delphi and taken over the oracle.

" And to this day the people of Delphi send high-born boys in procession there. And they, when they have reached Tempe and made a splendid sacrifice return back, after wearing themselves wreaths from the very laurel from which the god made himself a wreath."

We are inclined to think of the Greeks as a people apt to indulge in the singular practice of wearing wreaths in public, a practice among us confined to children on their birthdays and a few eccentric people on their wedding days. We forget the intensely practical purport of the custom. The ancient Greeks wore wreaths and carried boughs, not because they were artistic or poetical, but because they were ritualists, that they might bring back the spring and carry in the summer. The Greek bridegroom to-day, as well as the Greek bride, wears a wreath, that his marriage may be the beginning of new life, that his " wife may be as the fruitful vine, and his children as the olive branches round about his table." And our children to-day, though they do not know it, wear wreaths on their birthdays because with each new year their life is re-born.

Apollo then, was, like Dionysos, King of the May and—saving his presence—Jack-in-the-Green. The god manifestly arose out of the rite. For a moment let us see *how* he arose. It will be remembered that in a previous chapter (p. 70) we spoke of " personification."

We think of the god Apollo as an abstraction,
an unreal thing, perhaps as a "false god."
The god Apollo does not, and never did, exist.
He is an idea—a thing made by the imagination. But primitive man does not deal with
abstractions, does not worship them. What
happens is, as we saw (p. 71), something like
this : Year by year a boy is chosen to carry the
laurel, to bring in the May, and later year by
year a puppet is made. It is a different boy
each year, carrying a different laurel branch.
And yet in a sense it is the same boy; he is
always the Laurel-Bearer—" Daphnephoros,"
always the "Luck" of the village or city.
This Laurel-Bearer, the same yesterday, to-
day, and forever, is the stuff of which the
god is made. The god arises from the rite,
he is gradually detached from the rite, and
as soon as he gets a life and being of his own,
apart from the rite, he is a first stage in art,
a work of art existing in the mind, gradually
detached from even the faded action of ritual,
and later to be the model of the actual work
of art, the copy in stone.

The stages, it would seem, are : actual life
with its motor reactions, the ritual copy of
life with its faded reactions, the image of the

god projected by the rite, and, last, the copy of that image, the work of art.

We see now why in the history of all ages and every place art is what is called the "handmaid of religion." She is not really the "handmaid" at all. She springs straight out of the rite, and her first outward leap is the image of the god. Primitive art in Greece, in Egypt, in Assyria,[1] represents either rites, processions, sacrifices, magical ceremonies, embodied prayers; or else it represents the images of the gods who spring from those rites. Track any god right home, and you will find him lurking in a ritual sheath, from which he slowly emerges, first as a *dæmon*, or spirit, of the year, then as a full-blown divinity.

In Chapter II we saw how the *dromenon* gave birth to the *drama*, how, bit by bit, out of the chorus of dancers some dancers with-

[1] It is now held by some and good authorities that the prehistoric paintings of cave-dwelling man had also a ritual origin; that is, that the representations of animals were intended to act magically, to increase the "supply of the animal or help the hunter to catch him." But, as this question is still pending, I prefer, tempting though they are, not to use prehistoric paintings as material for my argument.

drew and became spectators sitting apart, and
on the other hand others of the dancers drew
apart on to the stage and presented to the
spectators a spectacle, a thing to be looked
at, not joined *in*. And we saw how in this
spectacular mood, this being cut loose from
immediate action, lay the very essence of the
artist and the art-lover. Now in the drama
of Thespis there was at first, we are told, but
one actor; later Æschylus added a second.
It is clear who this actor, this *protagonist* or
" first contender " was, the one actor with
the double part, who was Death to be carried
out and Summer to be carried in. He was
the Bough-Bearer, the only possible actor
in the one-part play of the renewal of life
and the return of the year.

The May-King, the leader of the choral
dance gave birth not only to the first actor
of the drama, but also, as we have just seen,
to the god, be he Dionysos or be he Apollo;
and this figure of the god thus imagined out
of the year-spirit was perhaps more fertile
for art than even the protagonist of the
drama. It may seem strange to us that a
god should rise up out of a dance or a pro-

cession, because dances and processions are
not an integral part of our national life, and
do not call up any very strong and instant
emotion. The old instinct lingers, it is true,
and emerges at critical moments; when a
king dies we form a great procession to carry
him to the grave, but we do not dance. We
have court balls, and these with their stately
ordered ceremonials are perhaps the last
survival of the genuinely civic dance, but a
court ball is not given at a king's funeral nor
in honour of a god.

But to the Greek the god and the dance
were never quite sundered. It almost seems
as if in the minds of Greek poets and philo-
sophers there lingered some dim half-conscious
remembrance that some of these gods at
least actually came out of the ritual dance.
Thus, Plato,[1] in treating of the importance
of rhythm in education says: " The gods,
pitying the toilsome race of men, have appointed the sequence of religious festivals to
give them times of rest, and have given them
the Muses and Apollo, the Muse-Leader, as
fellow-revellers."

" The young of all animals," he goes on to

[1] *Laws*, 653.

say, "cannot keep quiet, either in body or voice. They must leap and skip and over-flow with gamesomeness and sheer joy, and they must utter all sorts of cries. But whereas animals have no perception of order or disorder in their motions, the gods who have been appointed to men as our fellow-dancers have given to us a sense of pleasure in rhythm and harmony. And so they move us and lead our bands, knitting us together with songs and in dances, and these we call *choruses.*" Nor was it only Apollo and Dionysos who led the dance. Athena herself danced the Pyrrhic dance. " Our virgin lady," says Plato, " delighting in the sports of the dance, thought it not meet to dance with empty hands; she must be clothed in full armour, and in this attire go through the dance. And youths and maidens should in every respect imitate her example, honouring the goddess, both with a view to the actual necessities of war and to the festivals."

Plato is unconsciously inverting the order of things, natural happenings. Take the armed dance. There is, first, the " actual necessity of war." Men go to war armed, to

face actual dangers, and at their head is a
leader in full armour. That is real life. There
is then the festal re-enactment of war, when
the fight is not actually fought, but there is
an imitation of war. That is the ritual stage,
the *dromenon*. Here, too, there is a leader.
More and more this dance becomes a spectacle,
less and less an action. Then from the
periodic *dromenon*, the ritual enacted year by
year, emerges an imagined permanent leader;
a dæmon, or god—a Dionysos, an Apollo, an
Athena. Finally the account of what actually
happens is thrown into the past, into a
remote distance, and we have an "ætio-
logical" myth—a story told to give a cause
or reason. The whole natural process is
inverted.

And last, as already seen, the god, the first
work of art, the thing unseen, imagined out
of the ritual of the dance, is cast back into
the visible world and fixed in space. Can
we wonder that a classical writer [1] should
say " the statues of the craftsmen of old times
are the relics of ancient dancing." That is
just what they are, rites caught and fixed
and frozen. "Drawing," says a modern

[1] *Athen.* XIV, 26, p. 629.

critic,[1] " is at bottom, like all the arts, a kind of gesture, a method of dancing on paper." Sculpture, drawing, all the arts save music are imitative; so was the dance from which they sprang. But imitation is not all, or even first. " The dance may be mimetic; but the beauty and verve of the performance, not closeness of the imitation impresses; and tame additions of truth will encumber and not convince. The dance must control the pantomime." Art, that is, gradually dominates mere ritual.

We come to another point. The Greek gods as we know them in classical sculpture are always imaged in human shape. This was not of course always the case with other nations. We have seen how among savages the totem, that is, the emblem of tribal unity, was usually an animal or a plant. We have seen how the emotions of the Siberian tribe in Saghalien focussed on a bear. The savage totem, the Saghalien Bear, is on the way to be, but is not quite, a god; he is not personal enough. The Egyptians, and in

[1] D. S. MacColl, " A Year of Post-Impressionism " *Nineteenth Century*, p. 29. (1912.)

part the Assyrians, halted half-way and made
their gods into monstrous shapes, half-animal,
half-man, which have their own mystical
grandeur. But since we are men ourselves,
feeling human emotion, if our gods are in
great part projected emotions, the natural
form for them to take is human shape.

"Art imitates Nature," says Aristotle, in
a phrase that has been much misunderstood.
It has been taken to mean that art is a copy
or reproduction of natural objects. But by
"Nature" Aristotle never means the outside world of created things, he means rather
creative force, what produces, not what has
been produced. We might almost translate
the Greek phrase, "Art, like Nature, creates
things," "Art acts like Nature in producing
things." These things are, first and foremost, human things, human action. The
drama, with which Aristotle is so much concerned, invents human action like real,
natural action. Dancing "imitates character,
emotion, action." Art is to Aristotle almost
wholly bound by the limitations of *human*
nature.

This is, of course, characteristically a Greek
limitation. "Man is the measure of all

things," said the old Greek sophist, but modern science has taught us another lesson. Man may be in the foreground, but the drama of man's life is acted out for us against a tremendous background of natural happenings : a background that preceded man and will outlast him; and this background profoundly affects our imagination, and hence our art. We moderns are in love with the background. Our art is a landscape art. The ancient landscape painter could not, or would not, trust the background to tell its own tale : if he painted a mountain he set up a mountain-god to make it real; if he outlined a coast he set human coast-nymphs on its shore to make clear the meaning.

Contrast with this our modern landscape, from which bit by bit the nymph has been wholly banished. It is the art of a stage, without actors, a scene which is all background, all suggestion. It is an art given us by sheer recoil from science, which has dwarfed actual human life almost to imaginative extinction.

" Landscape, then, offered to the modern imagination a scene empty of definite actors, superhuman or human, that yielded to reverie without challenge all that is in a moral without a creed, tension or ambush of the dark, threat of ominous gloom, the relenting and tender return or overwhelming outburst of light, the pageantry of clouds above a world turned quaker, the monstrous weeds of trees outside the town, the sea that is obstinately epic still." [1]

It was to this world of backgrounds that men fled, hunted by the sense of their own insignificance.

"Minds the most strictly bound in their acts by civil life, in their fancy by the shrivelled look of destiny under scientific speculation, felt on solitary hill or shore those tides of the blood stir again that are ruled by the sun and the moon and travelled as if to tryst where an apparition might take form. Poets ordained themselves to this vigil, haunters of a desert church, prompters of an elemental theatre, listeners in solitary places for intimations from a spirit in hiding; and painters followed the impulse of Wordsworth."

[1] D. S. MacColl, *Nineteenth Century Art*, p. 20. (1902.)

We can only see the strength and weakness of Greek sculpture, feel the emotion of which it was the utterance, if we realize clearly this modern spirit of the background. All great modern, and perhaps even ancient, poets are touched by it. Drama itself, as Nietzsche showed, "hankers after dissolution into mystery. Shakespeare would occasionally knock the back out of the stage with a window opening on the 'cloud-capp'd towers.'" But Maeterlinck is the best example, because his genius is less. He is the embodiment, almost the caricature, of a tendency.

"Maeterlinck sets us figures in the foreground only to launch us into that limbus. The supers jabbering on the scene are there, children of presentiment and fear, to make us aware of a third, the mysterious one, whose name is not on the bills. They come to warn us by the nervous check and hurry of their gossip of the approach of that background power. Omen after omen announces him, the talk starts and drops at his approach, a door shuts and the thrill of his passage is the play." [1]

[1] D. S. MacColl, *op. cit.*, p. 18.

It is, perhaps, the temperaments that are most allured and terrified by this art of the bogey and the background that most feel the need of and best appreciate the calm and level, rational dignity of Greek naturalism and especially the naturalism of Greek sculpture.

For it is naturalism, not realism, not imitation. By all manner of renunciations Greek sculpture is what it is. The material, itself marble, is utterly unlike life, it is perfectly cold and still, it has neither the texture nor the colouring of life. The story of Pygmalion who fell in love with the statue he had himself sculptured is as false as it is tasteless. Greek sculpture is the last form of art to incite physical reaction. It is remote almost to the point of chill abstraction. The statue in the round renounces not only human life itself, but all the natural background and setting of life. The statues of the Greek gods are Olympian in spirit as well as subject. They are like the gods of Epicurus, cut loose alike from the affairs of men, and even the ordered ways of Nature. So Lucretius [1] pictures them :

[1] II, 18.

" The divinity of the gods is revealed and
their tranquil abodes, which neither winds do
shake nor clouds drench with rains, nor snow
congealed by sharp frost harms with hoary
fall : an ever cloudless ether o'ercanopies them,
and they laugh with light shed largely around.
Nature, too, supplies all their wants, and
nothing ever impairs their peace of mind."

Greek art moves on through a long course
of technical accomplishment, of ever-increas-
ing mastery over materials and methods.
But this course we need not follow.   For our
argument the last word is said in the figures
of these Olympians translated into stone.
Born of pressing human needs and desires,
images projected by active and even anxious
ritual, they pass into the upper air and dwell
aloof, spectator-like and all but spectral.

CHAPTER VII

RITUAL, ART AND LIFE

In the preceding chapters we have seen ritual emerge from the practical doings of life. We have noted that in ritual we have the beginning of a detachment from practical ends; we have watched the merely emotional dance develop from an undifferentiated chorus into a spectacle performed by actors and watched by spectators, a spectacle cut off, not only from real life, but also from ritual issues; a spectacle, in a word, that has become an end in itself. We have further seen that the choral dance is an undifferentiated whole which later divides out into three clearly articulate parts, the artist, the work of art, the spectator or art lover. We are now in a position to ask what is the good of all this antiquarian enquiry ? Why is it, apart from the mere delight of scientific enquiry, important to have seen that art arose from ritual ?

The answer is simple—

The object of this book, as stated in the preface, is to try to throw some light on the function of art, that is on what it has done, and still does to-day, for life. Now in the case of a complex growth like art, it is rarely if ever possible to understand its function— what it does, how it works—unless we know something of how that growth began, or, if its origin is hid, at least of the simpler forms of activity that preceded it. For art, this earlier stage, this simpler form, which is indeed itself as it were an embryo and rudimentary art, we found to be—ritual.

Ritual, then, has not been studied for its own sake, still less for its connection with any particular dogma, though, as a subject of singular gravity and beauty, ritual is well worth a lifetime's study. It has been studied because ritual is, we believe, a frequent and perhaps universal transition stage between actual life and that peculiar contemplation of or emotion towards life which we call art. All our long examination of beast-dances, May-day festivals and even of Greek drama has had just this for its object—to make clear that art—save perhaps in a few specially gifted natures—did not arise straight out of life, but out of that collective emphasis of the needs and desires of life which we have agreed to call ritual.

Our formal argument is now over and ritual may drop out of the discussion. But we would guard against a possible misunderstanding. We would not be taken to imply that ritual is obsolete and must drop out of life, giving place to the art it has engendered. It may well be that, for certain temperaments, ritual is a perennial need. Natures specially gifted can live lives that are emotionally vivid, even in the rare high air of art or science; but many, perhaps most of us, breathe more freely in the *medium*, literally the *midway* space, of some collective ritual. Moreover, for those of us who are not artists or original thinkers the life of the imagination, and even of the emotions, has been perhaps too long lived at second hand, received from the artist ready made and felt. To-day, owing largely to the progress of science, and a host of other causes social and economic, life grows daily fuller and freer, and every manifestation of life is regarded with a new reverence. With this fresh outpouring of the spirit, this fuller consciousness of life, there comes a need for *first-hand* emotion and expression, and that expression is found for all classes in a revival of the ritual dance. Some of the strenuous, exciting, self-expressive dances of to-day are of the soil and some exotic, but, based as they mostly are on very primitive ritual, they stand as singular evidence of this real recurrent need. Art in these latter days goes back as it were on her own steps, recrossing the ritual bridge back to life.

It remains to ask what, in the light of this ritual origin, is the function of art? How do we relate it to other forms of life, to science, to religion, to morality, to philosophy? These are big-sounding questions, and towards their solution only hints here and there can be offered, stray thoughts that have grown up out of this study of ritual origins and which, because they have helped the writer, are offered, with no thought of dogmatism, to the reader.

We English are not supposed to be an artistic people, yet art, in some form or another, bulks large in the national life. We have theatres, a National Gallery, we have

art-schools, our tradesmen provide for us
" art-furniture," we even hear, absurdly
enough, of " art-colours." Moreover, all this
is not a matter of mere antiquarian interest,
we do not simply go and admire the beauty
of the past in museums; a movement towards
or about art is all alive and astir among us.
We have new developments of the theatre,
problem plays, Reinhardt productions, Gordon
Craig scenery, Russian ballets. We have new
schools of painting treading on each other's
heels with breathless rapidity : Impressionists,
Post-Impressionists, Futurists. Art—or at
least the desire for, the interest in, art—is
assuredly not dead.

Moreover, and this is very important, we
all feel about art a certain obligation, such as
some of us feel about religion. There is an
" ought " about it. Perhaps we do not really
care much about pictures and poetry and
music, but we feel we " ought to." In the
case of music it has happily been at last
recognized that if you have not an " ear "
you cannot care for it, but two generations
ago, owing to the unfortunate cheapness
and popularity of keyed instruments, it was
widely held that one half of humanity, the

feminine half, " ought " to play the piano. This " ought " is, of course, like most social " oughts," a very complex product, but its existence is well worth noting.

It is worth noting because it indicates a vague feeling that art has a real value, that art is not a mere luxury, nor even a rarefied form of pleasure. No one feels they *ought* to take pleasure in beautiful scents or in the touch of velvet; they either do or they don't. The first point, then, that must be made clear is that art is of real value to life in a perfectly clear biological sense; it invigorates, enhances, promotes actual, spiritual, and through it physical life.

This from our historical account we should at the outset expect, because we have seen art, by way of ritual, arose out of life. And yet the statement is a sort of paradox, for we have seen also that art differs from ritual just in this, that in art, whether of the spectator or the creator, the " motor reactions," *i. e.* practical life, the life of doing, is for the time checked. This is of the essence of the artist's vision, that he sees things detached and therefore more vividly, more completely, and in a different light. This is of the essence of the artist's emotion, that it is purified from personal desire.

But, though the artist's vision and emotion alike are modified, purified, they are not devitalized. Far from that, by detachment from action they are focussed and intensified. Life is enhanced, only it is a different kind of life, it is the life of the image-world, of the *ima*gination; it is the spiritual and human life, as differentiated from the life we share with animals. It is a life we all, as human beings, possess in some, but very varying, degrees; and the natural man will always view the spiritual man askance, because he is not "practical." But the life of imagination, cut off from practical reaction as it is, becomes in turn a motor-force causing new emotions, and so pervading the general life, and thus ultimately becoming "practical." No one function is completely cut off from another. The main function of art is probably to intensify and purify emotion, but it is substantially certain that, if we did not feel, we could not think and should not act. Still it remains true that, in artistic contemplation and in the realms of the artist's imagination not only are practical motor-reactions cut off, but intelligence is suffused in, and to some extent subordinated to, emotion.

One function, then, of art is to feed and nurture the imagination and the spirit, and thereby enhance and invigorate the whole of human life. This is far removed from the view that the end of art is to give pleasure. Art does usually cause pleasure, singular and intense, and to that which causes such pleasure we give the name of Beauty. But to produce and enjoy Beauty is not the function of art. Beauty—or rather, the sensation of Beauty—is what the Greeks. would call an *epigignomenon ti telos,* words hard to translate, something between a by-product and a supervening perfection, a thing like—as Aristotle [1] for once beautifully says of pleasure—"the bloom of youth to a healthy young body."

That this is so we see most clearly in the simple fact that, when the artist begins to aim direct at Beauty, he usually misses it. We all know, perhaps by sad experience, that the man who seeks out pleasure for herself fails to find her. Let him do his work

[1] *Ethics,* X, 4.

well for that work's sake, exercise his faculties, " energize " as Aristotle would say, and he will find pleasure come out unawares to meet him with her shining face; but let him look for her, think of her, even desire her, and she hides her head. A man goes out hunting, thinks of nothing but following the hounds and taking his fences, being in at the death : his day is full—alas ! of pleasure, though he has scarcely known it. Let him forget the fox and the fences, think of pleasure, desire her, and he will be in at pleasure's death.

So it is with the artist. Let him feel strongly, and see raptly—that is, in complete detachment. Let him cast this, his rapt vision and his intense emotion, into outside form, a statue or a painting; that form will have about it a nameless thing, an unearthly aroma, which we call beauty; this nameless presence will cause in the spectator a sensation too rare to be called pleasure, and we shall call it a " sense of beauty." But let the artist aim direct at Beauty, and she is gone, gone before we hear the flutter of her wings.

The sign manual, the banner, as it were, of artistic creation is for the creative artist not

pleasure, but something better called joy.
Pleasure, it has been well said, is no more
than an instrument contrived by Nature to
obtain from the individual the preservation
and the propagation of life. True joy is not
the lure of life, but the consciousness of the
triumph of creation. Wherever joy is, creation
has been.[1] It may be the joy of a mother
in the physical creation of a child; it may be
the joy of the merchant adventurer in pushing out new enterprise, or of the engineer in
building a bridge, or of the artist in a master-
piece accomplished; but it is always of the
thing created. Again, contrast joy with
glory. Glory comes with success and is
exceedingly *pleasant ;* it is not joyous. Some
men say an artist's crown is glory; his
deepest satisfaction is in the applause of his
fellows. There is no greater mistake; we
care for praise just in proportion as we are
not sure we have succeeded. To the real
creative artist even praise and glory are
swallowed up in the supreme joy of creation.
Only the artist himself feels the real divine
fire, but it flames over into the work of art,

[1] H. Bergson, *Life and Consciousness*, Huxley Lecture,
May 29, 1911.

and even the spectator warms his hands at the glow.

We can now, I think, understand the difference between the artist and true lover of art on the one hand, and the mere æsthete on the other. The æsthete does not produce, or, if he produces, his work is thin and scanty. In this he differs from the artist; he does not feel so strongly and see so clearly that he is forced to utterance. He has no joy, only pleasure. He cannot even feel the reflection of this creative joy. In fact, he does not so much feel as want to feel. He seeks for pleasure, for sensual pleasure as his name says, not for the grosser kinds, but for pleasure of that rarefied kind that we call a sense of beauty. The æsthete, like the flirt, is cold. It is not even that his senses are easily stirred, but he seeks the sensation of stirring, and most often feigns it, not finds it. The æsthete is no more released from his own desires than the practical man, and he is without the practical man's healthy outlet in action. He sees life, not indeed in relation to action, but to his own personal sensation. By this alone he is debarred for ever from being an artist. As M. André Beaunier has well observed, by the irony of things, when we see life in relation to ourselves we cannot really represent it at all. The profligate thinks he knows women. It is his irony, his curse that, because he sees them always in relation to his own desires, his own pleasure, he never really knows them at all.

There is another important point. We have seen that art promotes a part of life, the spiritual, image-making side. But this side, wonderful though it is, is never the whole of actual life. There is always the practical side. The artist is always also a man. Now the æsthete tries to make his whole attitude artistic—that is, contemplative. He is always looking and prying and savouring, *savourant*, as he would say, when he ought to be living. The result is that there is nothing to *savourer*. All art springs by way of ritual out of keen emotion towards life, and even the power to appreciate art needs this emotional reality in the spectator. The æsthete leads at best a parasite, artistic life, dogged always by death and corruption.

This brings us straight on to another question : What about Art and Morality ?

Is Art immoral, or non-moral, or highly moral ? Here again public opinion is worth examining. Artists, we are told, are bad husbands, and they do not pay their debts. Or if they become good husbands and take to paying their debts, they take also to wallowing in domesticity and produce bad art or none at all; they get tangled in the machinery of practical reactions. Art, again, is apt to deal with risky subjects. Where should we be if there were not a Censor of Plays ? Many of these instructive attitudes about artists as immoral or non-moral, explain themselves instantly if we remember that the artist is *ipso facto* detached from practical life. In so far as he is an artist, for each and every creative moment he is inevitably a bad husband, if being a good husband means constant attention to your wife and her interests. Spiritual creation *à deux* is a happening so rare as to be negligible.

The remoteness of the artist, his essential inherent detachment from motor-reaction, explains the perplexities of the normal censor. He, being a " practical man," regards emotion and vision, feeling and ideas, as leading to action. He does not see that art arises out

of ritual and that even ritual is one remove
from practical life. In the censor's world
the spectacle of the nude leads straight to
desire, so the dancer must be draped; the
problem-play leads straight to the Divorce
Court, therefore it must be censored. The
normal censor apparently knows nothing of
that world where motor-reactions are cut
off, that house made without hands, whose
doors are closed on desire, eternal in the
heavens. The censor is not for the moment
a *persona grata*, but let us give him his due.
He acts according to his lights and these
often quite adequately represent the average
darkness. A normal audience contains many
" practical " men whose standard is the
same as that of the normal censor. Art—that
is vision detached from practical reactions—
is to them an unknown world full of moral
risks from which the artist is *quâ* artist
immune.

So far we might perhaps say that art was
non-moral. But the statement would be
misleading, since, as we have seen, art is
in its very origin social, and social means
human and collective. Moral and social are,
in their final analysis, the same. That human,

collective emotion, out of which we have seen
the choral dance arise, is in its essence moral;
that is, it unites. "Art," says Tolstoy, "has
this characteristic, that it unites people."
In this conviction, as we shall later see, he
anticipates the modern movement of the
Unanimists (p. 249).

But there is another, and perhaps simpler,
way in which art is moral. As already suggested, it purifies by cutting off the motor-
reactions of personal desire. An artist deeply
in love with his friend's wife once said : " If
only I could paint her and get what I want
from her, I could bear it." His wish strikes
a chill at first; it sounds egotistic; it has the
peculiar, instinctive, inevitable cruelty of the
artist, seeing in human nature material for
his art. But it shows us the moral side of
art. The artist was a good and sensitive man;
he saw the misery he had brought and would
bring to people he loved, and he saw, or rather
felt, a way of escape; he saw that through
art, through vision, through detachment,
desire might be slain, and the man within
him find peace. To some natures this instinct after art is almost their sole morality.
If they find themselves intimately entangled

in hate or jealousy or even contempt, so that
they are unable to see the object of their hate
or jealousy or contempt in a clear, quiet and
lovely light, they are restless, miserable,
morally out of gear, and they are constrained
to fetter or slay personal desire and so find
rest.

This aloofness, this purgation of emotion
from personal passion, art has in common
with philosophy. If the philosopher will
seek after truth, there must be, says Plotinus,
a " turning away " of the spirit, a detachment. He must aim at contemplation;
action, he says, is " a weakening of contemplation." Our word *theory*, which we use in
connection with reasoning and which comes
from the same Greek root as *theatre*, means
really looking fixedly at, contemplation; it
is very near in meaning to our *imagination*.
But the philosopher differs from the artist
in this : he aims not only at the contemplation of truth, but at the ordering of truths, he
seeks to make of the whole universe an in-
telligible structure. Further, he is not driven
by the gadfly of creation, he is not forced to
cast his images into visible or audible shape.

He is remoter from the push of life. Still, the philosopher, like the artist, lives in a world of his own, with a spell of its own near akin to beauty, and the secret of that spell is the same detachment from the tyranny of practical life. The essence of art, says Santayana, is " the steady contemplation of things in their order and worth." He might have been defining philosophy.

If art and philosophy are thus near akin, art and science are in their beginning, though not in their final development, contrasted. Science, it seems, begins with the desire for practical utility. Science, as Professor Bergson has told us, has for its initial aim the making of tools for life. Man tries to find out the laws of Nature, that is, how natural things behave, in order primarily that he may get the better of them, rule over them, shape them to his ends. That is why science is at first so near akin to magic—the cry of both is :

" I'll do, I'll do, and I'll do."

But, though the feet of science are thus firmly planted on the solid ground of practical action,

her head, too, sometimes touches the highest
heavens. The real man of science, like the
philosopher, soon comes to seek truth and
knowledge for their own sake. In art, in
science, in philosophy, there come eventually
the same detachment from personal desire
and practical reaction; and to artist, man of
science, and philosopher alike, through this
detachment there comes at times the same
peace that passeth all understanding.

Attempts have been often made to claim
for art the utility, the tool-making property,
that characterizes the beginnings of science.
Nothing is beautiful, it is sometimes said,
that is not useful; the beauty of a jug or a
table depends, we are often told, on its perfect
adaptation to its use. There is here some
confusion of thought and some obvious,
but possibly unconscious, special pleading.
Much of art, specially decorative art, arises
out of utilities, but its aim and its criterion
is not utility. Art may be structural, commemorative, magical, what-not, may grow up
out of all manner of practical needs, but it
is not till it is cut loose from these practical
needs that Art is herself and comes to her
own. This does not mean that the jugs or

tables are to be bad jugs or tables, still less
does it mean that the jugs or tables should
be covered with senseless machine-made ornament; but the utility of the jug or table is a
good in itself independent of, though often
associated with, its merit as art.

No one has, I think, ever called Art " the
handmaid of Science." There is, indeed, no
'need to establish a hierarchy. Yet in a sense
the converse is true and Science is the handmaid of Art. Art is only practicable as we
have seen, when it is possible safely to cut off
motor-reactions. By the long discipline of
ritual man accustomed himself to slacken his
hold on action, and be content with a shadowy
counterfeit practice. Then last, when through
knowledge he was relieved from the need of
immediate reaction to imminent realities, he
loosed hold for a moment altogether, and was
free to look, and art was born. He can never
quit his hold for long; but it would seem that,
as science advances and life gets easier and
easier, safer and safer, he may loose his hold
for longer spaces. Man subdues the world
about him first by force and then by reason;
and when the material world is mastered and
lies at his beck, he needs brute force no longer,

and needs reason no more to make tools for conquest. He is free to think for thought's sake, he may trust intuition once again, and above all dare to lose himself in contemplation, dare to be more and more an artist. Only here there lurks an almost ironical danger. Emotion towards life is the primary stuff of which art is made; there might be a shortage of this very emotional stuff of which art herself is ultimately compacted.

Science, then, helps to make art possible by making life safer and easier, it " makes straight in the desert a highway for our God." But only rarely and with special limitations easily understood does it provide actual material for art. Science deals with abstractions, concepts, class names, made by the intellect for convenience, that we may handle life on the side desirable to us. When we classify things, give them class-names, we simply mean that we note for convenience that certain actually existing objects have similar qualities, a fact it is convenient for us to know and register. These class-names being *abstract*—that is, bundles of qualities rent away from living actual objects, do not easily stir emotion, and, therefore, do not

easily become material for art whose function
it is to express and communicate emotion.
Particular qualities, like love, honour, faith,
may and *do* stir emotion; and certain bundles
of qualities like, for example, motherhood tend
towards personification; but the normal class
label like horse, man, triangle does not easily
become material for art; it remains a practical
utility for science.

The abstractions, the class-names of
science are in this respect quite different
from those other abstractions or unrealities
already studied—the gods of primitive religion. The very term we use shows this.
Abstractions are things, qualities, *dragged
away* consciously by the intellect, from actual
things objectively existing. The primitive
gods are personifications—*i. e.* collective
emotions taking shape in imagined form.
Dionysos has no more actual, objective existence than the abstract horse. But the god
Dionysos was not made by the intellect for
practical convenience, he was begotten by
emotion, and, therefore, he re-begets it. He
and all the other gods are, therefore, the
proper material for art; he is, indeed, one of
the earliest forms of art. The abstract horse,

on the other hand, is the outcome of reflection. We must honour him as of quite extraordinary use for the purposes of practical life, but he leaves us cold and, by the artist, is best neglected.

There remains the relation of Art to Religion.[1] By now, it may be hoped, this relation is transparently clear. The whole object of the present book has been to show how primitive art grew out of ritual, how art is in fact but a later and more sublimated, more detached form of ritual. We saw further that the primitive gods themselves were but projections or, if we like it better, personifications of the rite. They arose straight out of it.

Now we say advisedly " primitive gods," and this with no intention of obscurantism. The god of later days, the unknown source of life, the unresolved mystery of the world, is not begotten of a rite, is not, essentially not, the occasion or object of art. With his relation to art—which is indeed practically non-existent—we have nothing to do. Of the other

[1] Religion is here used as meaning the worship of some form of god, as the practical counterpart of theology.

gods we may safely say that not only are they
objects of art, they are its prime material; in
a word, primitive theology is an early stage in
the formation of art. Each primitive god,
like the rite from which he sprang, is a half-
way house between practical life and art; he
comes into being from a half, but only half,
inhibited desire.

Is there, then, no difference, except in
degree of detachment, between religion and
art? Both have the like emotional power;
both carry with them a sense of obligation,
though the obligation of religion is the
stronger. But there is one infallible criterion
between the two which is all-important, and
of wide-reaching consequences. Primitive
religion asserts that her imaginations have
objective existence; art more happily makes
no such claim. The worshipper of Apollo
believes, not only that he has imagined the
lovely figure of the god and cast a copy of
its shape in stone, but he also believes that
in the outside world the god Apollo exists as
an object. Now this is certainly untrue;
that is, it does not correspond with fact.
There is no such thing as the god Apollo, and

science makes a clean sweep of Apollo and
Dionysos and all such fictitious objectivities;
they are *eidola*, idols, phantasms, not objective
realities.   Apollo fades earlier than Dionysos
because the worshipper of Dionysos keeps
hold of *the* reality that he and his church or
group have projected the god.   He knows
that *prier, c'est élaborer Dieu ;* or, as he would
put it, he is " one with " his god.   Religion
has this in common with art, that it discredits
the actual practical world; but only because
it creates a new world and insists on its
actuality and objectivity.

Why does the conception of a god impose
obligation ?   Just because and in so far as
he claims to have objective existence.   By
giving to his god from the outset objective
existence the worshipper prevents his god
from taking his place in that high kingdom of spiritual realities which is the
imagination, and sets him down in that lower
objective world which always compels practical reaction.   What might have been an
ideal becomes an idol.   Straightway this ob-
jectified idol compels all sorts of ritual reactions
of prayer and praise and sacrifice.   It is
as though another and a more exacting and

commanding fellow-man were added to the universe. But a moment's reflection will show that, when we pass from the vague sense of power or *mana* felt by the savage to the personal god, to Dionysos or Apollo, though it may seem a set back it is a real advance. It is the substitution of a human and tolerably humane power for an incalculable whimsical and often cruel force. The idol is a step towards, not a step from, the ideal. Ritual makes these idols, and it is the business of science to shatter them and set the spirit free for contemplation. Ritual must wane that art may wax.

But we must never forget that ritual is the bridge by which man passes, the ladder by which he climbs from earth to heaven. The bridge must not be broken till the transit is made. And the time is not yet. We must not pull down the ladder till we are sure the last angel has climbed. Only then, at last, we dare not leave it standing. Earth pulls hard, and it may be that the angels who ascended might *de*scend and be for ever fallen.

It may be well at the close of our enquiry to test the conclusions at which we have arrived by comparing them with certain *endoxa*, as Aristotle would call them, that is, opinions and theories actually current at the present moment. We take these contemporary controversies, not implying that they are necessarily of high moment in the history of art, or that they are in any fundamental sense new discoveries; but because they are at this moment current and vital, and consequently form a good test for the adequacy of our doctrines. It will be satisfactory if we find our view includes these current opinions, even if it to some extent modifies them and, it may be hoped, sets them in a new light.

We have already considered the theory that holds art to be the creation or pursuit or enjoyment of beauty. The other view falls readily into two groups :

(1) The " imitation " theory, with its modification, the idealization theory, which holds that art either copies Nature, or, out of natural materials, improves on her.

(2) The " expression " theory, which holds that the aim of art is to express the emotions and thoughts of the artist.

The " Imitation " theory is out of fashion now-a-days. Plato and Aristotle held it; though Aristotle, as we have seen, did not mean by " imitating Nature " quite what we mean to-day. The Imitation theory began to die down with the rise of Romanticism, which stressed the personal, individual emotion of the artist. Whistler dealt it a rude, ill-considered blow by his effective, but really foolish and irrelevant, remark that to attempt to create Art by imitating Nature was " like trying to make music by sitting on the piano." But, as already noted, the Imitation theory of art was really killed by the invention of photography. It was impossible for the most insensate not to see that in a work of art, of sculpture or painting, there was an element of value not to be found in the exact transcript of a photograph. Henceforth the Imitation theory lived on only in the weakened form of Idealization.

The reaction against the Imitation theory has naturally and inevitably gone much too far. We have " thrown out the child with the bath-water." All through the present book we have tried to show that art *arises from* ritual, and ritual is in its essence a faded

action, an imitation. Moreover, every work
of art *is* a copy of something, only not a copy
of anything having actual existence in the
outside world.   Rather it is a copy of that
inner and highly emotionalized vision of the
artist which it is granted to him to see and
recreate when he is released from certain
practical reactions.

The Impressionism that dominated the
pictorial art of the later years of the nineteenth century was largely a modified and very
delicate imitation. Breaking with conventions
as to how things are *supposed to be*—conventions mainly based not on seeing but on
knowing or imagining—the Impressionist insists on purging his vision from knowledge,
and representing things not as they are but
as they really *look*. He imitates Nature not
as a whole, but as she presents herself to his
eyes. It was a most needful and valuable
purgation, since painting is the art proper of
the eye. But, when the new effects of the
world as simply *seen*, the new material of
light and shadow and tone, had been to some
extent—never completely—mastered, there
was inevitable reaction. Up sprang Post-

Impressionists and Futurists. They will not gladly be classed together, but both have this in common—they are Expressionists, not Impressionists, not Imitators.

The Expressionists, no matter by what name they call themselves, have one criterion. They believe that art is not the copying or idealizing of Nature, or of any aspect of Nature, but the expression and communication of the artist's emotion. We can see that, between them and the Imitationists, the Impressionists form a delicate bridge. They, too, focus their attention on the artist rather than the object, only it is on the artist's particular *vision*, his impression, what he actually sees, not on his emotion, what he feels.

Modern life is *not* simple—cannot be simple —ought not to be; it is not for nothing that we are heirs to the ages. Therefore the art that utters and expresses our emotion towards modern life cannot be simple; and, moreover, it must before all things embody not only that living tangle which is felt by the Futurists as so real, but it must purge and order it, by complexities of tone and rhythm hitherto unattempted. One art, beyond all others, has blossomed into real, spontaneous, unconscious life to-day, and that is Music; the other arts stand round arrayed, half paralyzed, with drooping, empty hands. The nineteenth century saw vast developments in an art that could express abstract, unlocalized, unpersonified feelings more completely than painting or poetry, the art of Music.

As a modern critic [1] has well observed : " In tone and rhythm music has a notation for every kind and degree of action and passion, presenting abstract moulds of its excitement, fluctuation, suspense, crisis, appeasement; and all this *anonymously*, without place, actors, circumstances, named or described, without a word spoken. Poetry has to supply definite thought, arguments driving at a conclusion, ideas mortgaged to this or that creed or system; and to give force to these can command only a few rhythms limited by the duration of a human breath and the pitch of an octave. The little effects worked out in this small compass music sweeps up and builds into vast fabrics of emotion with a dissolute freedom undreamed of in any other art."

[1] Mr. D. S. MacColl.

It may be that music provides for a century too stagnant and listless to act out its own emotions, too reflective to be frankly sensuous, a shadowy pageant of sense and emotion, that serves as a *katharsis* or purgation.

Anyhow, " an art that came out of the old world two centuries ago, with a few chants, love-songs, and dances; that a century ago was still tied to the words of a mass or an opera; or threading little dance-movements together in a ' suite,' became in the last century this extraordinary debauch, in which the man who has never seen a battle, loved a woman, or worshipped a god, may not only ideally, but through the response of his nerves and pulses to immediate rhythmical attack, enjoy the ghosts of struggle, rapture, and exaltation with a volume and intricacy, an anguish, a triumph, an irresponsibility, unheard of. An amplified pattern of action and emotion is given : each man may fit to it what images he will." [1]

If our contention throughout this book be correct the Expressionists are in one matter abundantly right. Art, we have seen, again

[1] D. S. MacColl, *Nineteenth Century Art*, p. 21. (1902.)

and again rises by way of ritual out of emotion, out of life keenly and vividly livid. The younger generation are always talking of life; they have a sort of cult of life. Some of the more valorous spirits among them even tend to disparage art that life may be the more exalted. " Stop painting and sculping," they cry, " and go and see a football match." There you have life ! Life is, undoubtedly, essential to art because life is the stuff of emotion, but some thinkers and artists have an oddly limited notion of what life is. It must, it seems, in the first place, be essentially physical. To sit and dream in your study is not to live. The reason of this odd limitation is easy to see. We all think life is especially the sort of life we are *not* living ourselves. The hard-worked University professor thinks that " Life " is to be found in a French *café ;* the polished London journalist looks for " Life " among the naked Polynesians. The cult of savagery, and even of simplicity, in every form, simply spells complex civilization and diminished physical vitality.

The Expressionist is, then, triumphantly right in the stress he lays on emotion; but he is not right if he limits life to certain of its more elementary manifestations; and still less is he right, to our minds, in making life and art in any sense coextensive. Art, as we have seen, sustains and invigorates life, but only does it by withdrawal from these very same elementary forms of life, by inhibiting certain sensuous reactions.

In another matter one section of Expressionists, the Futurists, are in the main right. The emotion to be expressed is the emotion of to-day, or still better to-morrow. The mimetic dance arose not only nor chiefly out of reflection on the past; but out of either immediate joy or imminent fear or insistent hope for the future. We are not prepared perhaps to go all lengths, to " burn all museums " because of their contagious corruption, though we might be prepared to " banish the nude for the space of ten years." If there is to be any true living art, it must arise, not from the contemplation of Greek statues, not from the revival of folk-songs, not even from the re-enacting of Greek plays, but from a keen emotion felt towards things and people living to-day, in modern conditions, including, among other and deeper forms of life, the haste and

hurry of the modern street, the whirr of motor
cars and aeroplanes.

There are artists alive to-day, strayed
revellers, who wish themselves back in the
Middle Ages, who long for the time when each
man would have his house carved with a bit
of lovely ornament, when every village church
had its Madonna and Child, when, in a word,
art and life and religion went hand in hand,
not sharply sundered by castes and pro-
fessions. But we may not put back the
clock, and, if by differentiation we lose something, we gain much. The old choral dance
on the orchestral floor was an undifferentiated
thing, it had a beauty of its own; but by its
differentiation, by the severance of artist and
actors and spectators, we have gained—the
drama. We may not cast reluctant eyes backwards; the world goes forward to new forms
of life, and the Churches of to-day must and
should become the Museums of to-morrow.

It is curious and instructive to note that
Tolstoy's theory of Art, though not his
practice, is essentially Expressive and even
approaches the dogmas of the Futurist. Art
is to him just the transmission of personal

emotion to others.   It may be bad emotion
or it may be good emotion, emotion it must
be.   To take his simple and instructive
instance : a boy goes out into a wood and
meets a wolf, he is frightened, he comes back
and tells the other villagers what he felt, how
he went to the wood feeling happy and light-
hearted and the wolf came, and what the wolf
looked like, and how he began to be frightened.
This is, according to Tolstoy, art.   Even if
the boy never saw a wolf at all, if he had really
at another time been frightened, and if he
was able to conjure up fear in himself and
communicate it to others—that also would be
art.   The essential is, according to Tolstoy,
that he should feel himself and so represent
his feeling that he communicates it to others.[1]
Art-schools, art-professionalism, art-criticism
are all useless or worse than useless, because
they cannot teach a man to feel.   Only life
can do that.

All art is, according to Tolstoy, good *quâ*

[1] It is interesting to find, since the above was written,
that the Confession of Faith published in the catalogue of
the Second Post-Impressionist Exhibition (1912, p. 21) reproduces, consciously or unconsciously, Tolstoy's view :
*We have ceased to ask, " What does this picture represent ? "
and ask instead, " What does it make us feel ? "*

art that succeeds in transmitting emotion. But there is good emotion and bad emotion, and the only right material for art is good emotion, and the only good emotion, the only emotion worth expressing, is subsumed, according to Tolstoy, in the religion of the day. This is how he explains the constant affinity in nearly all ages of art and religion. Instead of regarding religion as an early phase of art, he proceeds to define religious perception as the highest social ideal of the moment, as that " understanding of the meaning of life which represents the highest level to which men of that society have attained, an understanding defining the highest good at which that society aims." " Religious perception in a society," he beautifully adds, " is like the direction of a flowing river. If the river flows at all, it must have a direction." Thus, religion, to Tolstoy, is not dogma, not petrifaction, it makes indeed dogma impossible. The religious perception of to-day flows, Tolstoi says, in the Christian channel towards the union of man in a common brotherhood. It is the business of the modern artist to feel and transmit emotion towards this unity of man.

Now it is not our purpose to examine
whether Tolstoy's definition of religion is
adequate or indeed illuminating. What we
wish to note is that he grasps the truth that
in art we must look and feel, and look and
feel forward, not backward, if we would live.
Art somehow, like language, is always feeling
forward to newer, fuller, subtler emotions.
She seems indeed in a way to feel ahead even
of science; a poet will forecast dimly what a
later discovery will confirm. Whether and
how long old channels, old forms will suffice
for the new spirit can never be foreseen.

We end with a point of great importance,
though the doctrine we would emphasize
may be to some a hard saying, even a stum-
bling-block. Art, as Tolstoy divined, is social,
not individual. Art is, as we have seen,
social in origin, it remains and must remain
social in function. The dance from which
the drama rose was a choral dance, the dance
of a band, a group, a church, a community,
what the Greeks called a *thiasos*. The word
means a *band* and a *thing of devotion;* and
reverence, devotion, collective emotion, is
social in its very being. That band was, to

begin with, as we saw, the whole collection of initiated tribesmen, linked by a common name, rallying round a common symbol.

Even to-day, when individualism is rampant, art bears traces of its collective, social origin. We feel about it, as noted before, a certain " ought " which always spells social obligation. Moreover, whenever we have a new movement in art, it issues from a group, usually from a small professional coterie, but marked by strong social instincts, by a missionary spirit, by intemperate zeal in propaganda, by a tendency, always social, to crystallize conviction into dogma. We can scarcely, unless we are as high-hearted as Tolstoy, hope now-a-days for an art that shall be world-wide. The tribe is extinct, the family in its old rigid form moribund, the social groups we now look to as centres of emotion are the groups of industry, of professionalism and of sheer mutual attraction. Small and strange though such groups may appear, they are real social factors.

Now this social, collective element in art is too apt to be forgotten. When an artist claims that expression is the aim of art he is too apt to mean self-expression only—

utterance of individual emotion.   Utterance
of individual emotion is very closely neigh-
boured by, is almost identical with, self-
enhancement.   What should be a generous,
and in part altruistic, exaltation becomes
mere *megalomania*.   This egotism is, of course,
a danger inherent in all art.   The suspension
of motor-reactions to the practical world
isolates the artist, cuts him off from his
fellow-men, makes him in a sense an egotist.
Art, said Zola, is "the world seen through a
temperament."   But this suspension is, not
that he should turn inward to feed on his
own vitals, but rather to free him for contemplation.   All great art releases from self.

The young are often temporary artists : art,
being based on life, calls for a strong vitality.
The young are also self-centred and seek self-
enhancement.   This need of self-expression is
a sort of artistic impulse.   The young are,
partly from sheer immaturity, still more
through a foolish convention, shut out from
real life ; they are secluded, forced to become
in a sense artists, or, if they have not the
power for that, at least self-aggrandizers.
They write lyric poems, they love masquerad-

ing, they focus life on to themselves in a way which, later on, life itself makes impossible. This pseudo-art, this self-aggrandizement usually dies a natural death before the age of thirty. If it live on, one remedy is, of course, the scientific attitude; that attitude which is bent on considering and discovering the relations of things among themselves, not their personal relation to us. The study of science is a priceless discipline in self-abnegation, but only in negation; it looses us from self, it does not link us to others. The real and natural remedy for the egotism of youth is Life, not necessarily the haunting of *cafés*, or even the watching of football matches, but strenuous activity in the simplest human relations of daily happenings. " Whatsoever thy hand findeth to do, do it with thy might."

There is always apt to be some discord between the artist and the large practical world in which he lives, but those ages are happiest in which the discord is least. The nineteenth century, amid its splendid achievements in science and industry, in government and learning, and above all in humanity, illustrates this conflict in an interesting way.

To literature, an art which can explain itself, the great public world lent on the whole a reverent and intelligent ear. Its great prose writers were at peace with their audience and were inspired by great public interests. Some of the greatest, for example Tolstoy, produced their finest work on widely human subjects, and numbered their readers and admirers probably by the million. Writers like Dickens, Thackeray, Kingsley, Mill, and Carlyle, even poets like Tennyson and Browning, were full of great public interests and causes, and, in different degrees and at different stages of their lives, were thoroughly and immensely popular. On the other hand, one can find, at the beginning of the period, figures like Blake and Shelley, and all through it a number of painters —the pre-Raphaelites, the Impressionists— walking like aliens in a Philistine world. Even great figures like Burne-Jones and Whistler were for the greater part of their lives unrecognized or mocked at. Millais reached the attention of the world, but was thought by the stricter fraternity to have in some sense or other sold his soul and committed the great sin of considering the bourgeois. The bourgeois should be despised not partially but completely. His life, his interests, his code of ethics and conduct must all be matters of entire indifference or amused contempt, to the true artist who intends to do his own true work and call his soul his own.

At a certain moment, during the eighties and nineties, it looked as if these doctrines were generally accepted, and the divorce between art and the community had become permanent. But it seems as if this attitude, which coincided with a period of reaction in political matters and a recrudescence of a belief in force and on unreasoned authority, is already passing away. There are not wanting signs that art, both in painting and sculpture, and in poetry and novel-writing, is beginning again to realize its social function, beginning to be impatient of mere individual emotion, beginning to aim at something bigger, more bound up with a feeling towards and for the common weal.

Take work like that of Mr. Galsworthy or Mr. Masefield or Mr. Arnold Bennett. Without appraising its merits or demerits we cannot but note that the social sense is always there, whether it be of a class or of a whole community. In a play like *Justice* the writer

does not " express " himself, he does not
even merely show the pathos of a single
human being's destiny, he sets before us a
much bigger thing—man tragically caught
and torn in the iron hands of a man-made
machine, Society itself. Incarnate Law is
the protagonist, and, as it happens, the villain
of the piece. It is a fragment of *Les Misér-
ables* over again, in a severer and more
restrained technique. An art like this starts,
no doubt, from emotion towards personal
happenings—there is nothing else from which
it can start; but, even as it sets sail for wider
seas, it is loosed from personal moorings.

Science has given us back something
strangely like a World-Soul, and art is beginning to feel she must utter our emotion towards
it. Such art is exposed to an inherent and
imminent peril. Its very bigness and newness
tends to set up fresh and powerful reactions.
Unless, in the process of creation, these can
be inhibited, the artist will be lost in the
reformer, and the play or the novel turn
tract. This does not mean that the artist, if
he is strong enough, may not be reformer too,
only not at the moment of creation.

The art of Mr. Arnold Bennett gets its

bigness, its collectivity, in part—from extension over time. Far from seeking after beauty,
he almost goes out to embrace ugliness. He
does not spare us even dullness, that we may
get a sense of the long, waste spaces of life,
their dreary reality. We are keenly interested
in the loves of hero and heroine, but all the
time something much bigger is going on,
generation after generation rolls by in ceaseless panorama; it is the life not of Edwin and
Hilda, it is the life of the Five Towns. After
a vision so big, to come back to the ordinary
individualistic love-story is like looking
through the wrong end of a telescope.

Art of high quality and calibre is seldom
obscure. The great popular writers of the
nineteenth century — Dickens, Thackeray,
Tennyson, Tolstoy—wrote so that all could
understand. A really big artist has something
important to say, something vast to show,
something that moves him and presses on
him; and he will say it simply because he
must get it said. He will trick it out with
no devices, most of all with no obscurities.
It has vexed and torn him enough while it
was pushing its way to be born. He has no
peace till it is said, and said as clearly as he

may. He says it, not consciously for the
sake of others, but for himself, to ease him
from the burden of big thought. Moreover,
art, whose business is to transmit emotion,
should need no commentary. Art comes out
of *theoria*, contemplation, steady looking at,
but never out of *theory*. Theory can neither
engender nor finally support it. An exhibition of pictures with an explanatory catalogue,
scientifically interesting though it may be,
stands, in a sense, self-condemned.

We must, however, remember that all art
is not of the whole community. There are
small groups feeling their own small but
still collective emotion, fashioning their own
language, obscure sometimes to all but themselves. They are right so to fashion it, but,
if they appeal to a wider world, they must
strive to speak in the vulgar tongue, under-
standed of the people.

It is, indeed, a hopeful sign of the times, a
mark of the revival of social as contrasted
with merely individualistic instincts that
a younger generation of poets, at least in
France, tend to form themselves into small
groups, held together not merely by eccen-

tricities of language or garb, but by some deep
inner conviction strongly held in common.
Such a unity of spirit is seen in the works of
the latter group of thinkers and writers
known as *Unanimists*. They tried and failed
to found a community. Their doctrine, if
doctrine convictions so fluid can be called, is
strangely like the old group-religion of the
common dance, only more articulate. Of the
Unanimist it might truly be said, " *il buvait
l'indistinction.*" To him the harsh old Roman
mandate *Divide et impera*, "Divide men that
you may rule them," spells death. His dream
is not of empire and personal property but
of the realization of life, common to all. To
this school the great reality is the social group,
whatever form it take, family, village or town.
Their only dogma is the unity and immeasur-
able sanctity of life. In practice they are
Christian, yet wholly free from the asceticism
of modern Christianity. Their attitude in art is
as remote as possible from, it is indeed the very
antithesis to, the æsthetic exclusiveness of
the close of last century. Like St. Peter, the
Unanimists have seen a sheet let down and
heard a voice from heaven saying: " Call
thou nothing common nor unclean."

Above all, the Unanimist remembers and realizes afresh the old truth that " no man liveth unto himself." According to the Expressionist's creed, as we have seen, the end of art is to utter and communicate emotion. The fullest and finest emotions are those one human being feels towards another. Every sympathy is an enrichment of life, every antipathy a negation. It follows then, that, for the Unanimist, Love is the fulfilling of his Law.

It is a beautiful and life-giving faith, felt and with a perfect sincerity expressed towards all nature by the Indian poet Tagore, and towards humanity especially by M. Vildrac in his *Book of Love* ("Livre d'Amour"). He tells us in his "Commentary" how to-day the poet, sitting at home with pen and paper before him, feels that he is pent in, stifled by himself. He had been about to re-tell the old, old story of himself, to set himself once more on the stage of his poem—the same old dusty self tricked out, costumed anew. Suddenly he knows the figure to be tawdry and shameful. He is hot all over when he looks at it; he must out into the air, into the street, out of the stuffy museum where so long he has stirred the dead egotist ashes, out into the bigger life, the life of his fellows; he must live, with them, by them, in them.

"I am weary of deeds done inside myself,
  I am weary of voyages inside myself,
  And of heroism wrought by strokes of the
    pen,
  And of a beauty made up of formulæ.

"I am ashamed of lying to my work,
  Of my work lying to my life,
  And of being able to content myself,
  By burning sweet spices,
  With the mouldering smell that is master
    here."

Again, in "The Conquerors," the poet dreams of the Victorious One who has no army, the Knight who rides afoot, the Crusader without breviary or scrip, the Pilgrim of Love who, by the shining in his eyes, draws all men to him, and they in turn draw other men until, at last:

"The time came in the land,
  The time of the Great Conquest,

When the people with this desire
Left the threshold of their door
To go forth towards one another.

" And the time came in the land
When to fill all its story
There was nothing but songs in unison,
One round danced about the houses,
One battle and one victory."

And so our tale ends where it began, with
the Choral Dance.

BIBLIOGRAPHY

For Ancient and Primitive Ritual the best general book of reference is:

Frazer, J. G. *The Golden Bough*, 3rd edition, 1911, from which most of the instances in the present manual are taken. Part IV of *The Golden Bough*, i. e. the section dealing with *Adonis, Attis, and Osiris*, should especially be consulted.

Also an earlier, epoch-making book:

Robertson Smith, W. *Lectures on the Religion of the Semites*, 1889 [3rd edition, 1927]. For certain fundamental ritual notions, *e.g.* sacrifice, holiness, etc.

[For Egyptian and Babylonian ritual: *Myth and Ritual*, edited by S. H. Hooke, 1933.]

For the Greek Drama, as arising out of the ritual dance: Professor Gilbert Murray's *Excursus on the Ritual Forms preserved in Greek Tragedy* in J. E. Harrison's *Themis*, 1912, and pp. 327–40 in the same book; and for the religion of Dionysos and the drama, J. E. Harrison's *Prolegomena*, 1907, Chapters VIII and X. For the fusion of the ritual dance and hero-worship, see W. Leaf, *Homer and History*, 1915, Chapter VII. For a quite different view of drama as arising wholly from the worship of the dead, see Professor W. Ridgeway, *The Origin of Tragedy*, 1910. An important discussion of the relation of *tragedy* to the winter festival of the *Lenaia* appears in A. B. Cook's *Zeus*, vol. i, sec. 6 (xxi) [1914].

[More recent works on Greek drama: A. W. Pickard-Cambridge, *Dithyramb, Tragedy and Comedy*, 1927; G. Thomson, *Aeschylus and Athens*, 1941.]

For Primitive Art:

Hirn, Y. *The Origins of Art*, 1900. The main theory of the book the present writer believes to be inadequate, but it contains an excellent collection of facts relating to Art, Magic, Art and Work, Mimetic Dances, etc., and much valuable discussion of principles.

Grosse, E. *The Beginnings of Art*, 1897, in the Chicago Anthropological Series. Valuable for its full illustrations of primitive art, as well as for text.

[Boas, F., *Primitive Art*, 1927.]

254   BIBLIOGRAPHY

For the Theory of Art:

TOLSTOY, L. *What is Art?* Translated by Aylmer Maude, in the Scott Library.

FRY, ROGER E. *An Essay in Æsthetics*, in the *New Quarterly*, April 1909, p. 174.
This is the best general statement of the function of Art known to me. It should be read in connection with Mr. Bullough's article, quoted on p. 129, which gives the psychological basis of a similar view of the nature of art. My own theory was formulated independently, in relation to the development of the Greek theatre, but I am very glad to find that it is in substantial agreement with those of two such distinguished authorities on æsthetics. For my later conclusions on art, see *Alpha and Omega*, 1915, pp. 208–220.

[CAUDWELL, C., *Illusion and Reality*, 1937.]

For more advanced students:

DUSSAUZE, HENRI. *Les Règles esthétiques et les lois du sentiment*, 1911.

MÜLLER-FREIENFELS, R. *Psychologie der Kunst*, 1912.

INDEX